1st EDITION

Perspectives on Modern World History

The 1992 Los Angeles Riots

1st EDITION

Perspectives on Modern World History

The 1992 Los Angeles Riots

Louise I. Gerdes

Editor

GREENHAVEN PRESS
A part of Gale, Cengage Learning

GALE
CENGAGE Learning·

Farmington Hills, Mich • San Francisco • New York • Waterville, Maine
Meriden, Conn • Mason, Ohio • Chicago

GALE
CENGAGE Learning·

Elizabeth Des Chenes, *Director, Content Strategy*
Cynthia Sanner, *Publisher*
Douglas Dentino, *Manager, New Product*

WCN: 01-100-101

For more information, contact:
Greenhaven Press
27500 Drake Rd.
Farmington Hills, MI 48331-3535
Or you can visit our Internet site at gale.cengage.com.

For product information and technology assistance, contact us at
Gale Customer Support, 1-800-877-4253.

For permission to use material from this text or product, submit all requests online at
www.cengage.com/permissions.

Further permissions questions can be e-mailed to permissionrequest@cengage.com.

Articles in Greenhaven Press anthologies are often edited for length to meet page requirements. In addition, original titles of these works are changed to clearly present the main thesis and to explicitly indicate the author's opinion. Every effort is made to ensure that Greenhaven Press accurately reflects the original intent of the authors. Every effort has been made to trace the owners of copyrighted material.

Cover images © David Butow/Corbis and © Peter Turnley/Corbis.

LIBRARY OF CONGRESS CATALOGING-IN-PUBLICATION DATA

The 1992 Los Angeles riots / Louise I. Gerdes, book editor.
    pages cm -- (Perspectives on modern world history)
    Includes bibliographical references and index.
    ISBN 978-0-7377-7008-7 (hardcover)
  1. Rodney King Riots, Los Angeles, Calif., 1992. 2. Los Angeles (Calif.)--Race relations. 3. King, Rodney, 1965-2012. 4. Racism--California--Los Angeles. 5. Police misconduct--California--Los Angeles. 6. African Americans--California--Los Angeles. I. Gerdes, Louise I., 1953-, editor of compilation.
    F869.L89N414 2014
    979.4'94053--dc23
                                                                    2013036322

Printed in the United States of America
1 2 3 4 5 6 7 18 17 16 15 14

CONTENTS

American merchants who armed themselves
to defend against looters as vigilantes.

CHAPTER 3   ## Personal Narratives

in sadness as their city burned. That people are looking at the city's assets following the riots, however, inspires him.

FOREWORD

"History cannot give us a program for the future, but it can give us a fuller understanding of ourselves, and of our common humanity, so that we can better face the future."

—Robert Penn Warren,
American poet and novelist

The history of each nation is punctuated by momentous events that represent turning points for that nation, with an impact felt far beyond its borders. These events—displaying the full range of human capabilities, from violence, greed, and ignorance to heroism, courage, and strength—are nearly always complicated and multifaceted. Any student of history faces the challenge of grasping the many strands that constitute such world-changing events as wars, social movements, and environmental disasters. But understanding these significant historic events can be enhanced by exposure to a variety of perspectives, whether of people involved intimately or of ones observing from a distance of miles or years. Understanding can also be increased by learning about the controversies surrounding such events and exploring hot-button issues from multiple angles. Finally, true understanding of important historic events involves knowledge of the events' human impact—of the ways such events affected people in their everyday lives—all over the world.

Perspectives on Modern World History examines global historic events from the twentieth century onward by presenting analysis and observation from numerous vantage points. Each volume offers high school, early college level, and general interest readers a thematically

1

arranged anthology of previously published materials that address a major historical event, with an emphasis on international coverage. Each volume opens with background information on the event, then presents the controversies surrounding that event, and concludes with first-person narratives from people who lived through the event or were affected by it. By providing primary sources from the time of the event, as well as relevant commentary surrounding the event, this series can be used to inform debate, help develop critical thinking skills, increase global awareness, and enhance an understanding of international perspectives on history.

Material in each volume is selected from a diverse range of sources, including journals, magazines, newspapers, nonfiction books, personal narratives, speeches, congressional testimony, government documents, pamphlets, organization newsletters, and position papers. Articles taken from these sources are carefully edited and introduced to provide context and background. Each volume of Perspectives on Modern World History includes an array of views on events of global significance. Much of the material comes from international sources and from US sources that provide extensive international coverage.

Each volume in the Perspectives on Modern World History series also includes:

- A full-color **world map**, offering context and geographic perspective.
- An annotated **table of contents** that provides a brief summary of each essay in the volume.
- An **introduction** specific to the volume topic.
- For each viewpoint, a brief **introduction** that has notes about the author and source of the viewpoint, and that provides a summary of its main points.
- Full-color **charts**, **graphs**, **maps**, and other visual representations.

- Informational **sidebars** that explore the lives of key individuals, give background on historical events, or explain scientific or technical concepts.
- A **glossary** that defines key terms, as needed.
- A **chronology** of important dates preceding, during, and immediately following the event.
- A **bibliography** of additional books, periodicals, and websites for further research.
- A comprehensive **subject index** that offers access to people, places, and events cited in the text.

Perspectives on Modern World History is designed for a broad spectrum of readers who want to learn more about not only history but also current events, political science, government, international relations, and sociology—students doing research for class assignments or debates, teachers and faculty seeking to supplement course materials, and others wanting to improve their understanding of history. Each volume of Perspectives on Modern World History is designed to illuminate a complicated event, to spark debate, and to show the human perspective behind the world's most significant happenings of recent decades.

INTRODUCTION

Shortly after midnight on March 3, 1991, from his apartment in the Lake View Terrace community of Los Angeles, George Holliday filmed Los Angeles Police Department officers repeatedly striking an African American man with their batons. The next day, Holliday gave the videotape to the Los Angeles television station KTLA. After turning over a copy to the police, KTLA aired the video. The next day, CNN, the relatively new, but fast growing twenty-four-hour cable news network, obtained the tape and within days millions of Americans had watched the video of the beating of Rodney King over and over again. When on April 29, 1992, a jury acquitted four white police officers of what many Americans believed was a clear case of police brutality, many presumed that the only reason for such a verdict was racism. While few dispute that the April 29, 1992, acquittal was the spark that ignited the subsequent violence and destruction that erupted in Los Angeles, analysts disagree about the meaning of the riots that followed and thus how history should characterize these events. Indeed, whether what happened after the verdict was a race riot, an urban rebellion, a reaction to ethnic tension, or simply criminal opportunism is subject to vigorous debate.

During the violence, Americans were bombarded by images on television, in newspapers, and even in rap lyrics. For many, memory of those terrifying five days is framed by these images. These images are, however, incomplete, shaped by the cameraman, the writer, and the artist. *Los Angeles Times* book critic David L. Ulin, when comparing the literature that emerged from the 1965 Watts riots to the literature following the events of April 1992, reasons, "No equivalent sense of history emerges when we think about 1992. Instead, we are left with fragments, snapshots, the loose tiles of what former [Los Angeles] Mayor Tom Bradley liked to call 'the glorious mosaic,' which the riots revealed to be a lie." Despite the wide availability of these images—the home video of the Rodney King beating, the rhythmic forewarning of gangsta rap artists, the televised beating of truck driver Reginald Denny, stills of armed Korean American merchants wearing headbands, and front-page headlines, "A Long Night of Anger, Anarchy"—these image fragments alone are, in the eyes of some, inadequate to interpret the events. Nevertheless, for many, these images reflect the variety of perspectives on the meaning of the 1992 Los Angeles riots.

For those analysts who view the events that followed the verdict as a racial rebellion, the images of the Rodney King beating and the violence that followed provided Americans with context for the reaction. According to David A. Love, who writes for NBC's, *The Grio,* which focuses on news and issues of interest to African Americans, "Taken in isolation, riots may be dismissed solely as senseless and random acts of lawlessness, violence and mayhem. . . . But there was a context to what happened in South Central L.A.—the brutal beating of a black motorist by white police officers." Americans were able to see in the video what many African Americans had long claimed was true—justice for police abuses in black communities is difficult to achieve. Moreover, when Americans viewed those involved in the violence, they could see that race is not just a problem of black and white. He notes that 51 percent of the riot arrests were Latinos, and rioters often targeted Korean merchants. In Love's view, the rebellion provided a preview of what may come in an increasingly diverse nation: "For today's society—with its racial scapegoats, white conservative push back against Latino immigrants, war against ethnic studies and the surfacing of anti-Muslim, anti-Arab intolerance—the L.A. riots gave America a preview of the racial tensions to come."

If the images of the Rodney King beating provided context for the riots, some maintain that the often violent images of gangsta rap were a premonition. Indeed, "Loud, observant, and demanding of attention, gangsta rap, in particular, became soundtrack to this era of racial instability, and is believed by many to not only have led the nation in cultural exploration, but to have actually prophesized the insurrection," claims Courtney Garcia, another *Grio* writer. In his 1991 album *Death Certificate*, rap artist Ice Cube explores, in oftentimes violent musical images, problems that he believes led to the riots—systemic police brutality in black neighborhoods and tension with Korean merchants. Garcia interviewed the artist and actor on the riots' twentieth anniversary. According to Ice Cube, "The police really had carte blanche in our neighborhoods till we did the song 'F**k tha Police,' then people really started to actually look at what they were doing. And then the Rodney King incident came out to really show [it]. So, we had been talking about this all along." Once the violence and looting were over, rap artists continued to send messages about frustration in their neighborhoods like those expressed in Ice Cube's controversial song "We Had to Tear This Motherf**ker Up." However, Garcia suggests, these musical images may not have had the lasting impression rap artists hoped for. In Ice Cube's words, "I think we're sort of in the same place we were. I think that people make a lot of money on us being separated, and those people are still in power." In his song, "Wicked," Ice Cube predicts more violence to come.

Some commentators dispute the claim that televised images of the riots provided accurate context. They maintain that although the images showed the riots for what they were—the acts of ruthless criminals—the media commentary tainted these images with their lack of objectivity. "Their eyesight is disabled by their imagination," reasons conservative British journalist John O'Sullivan. He argues that the reporting that dominated the riot coverage suggested that the riots were a legitimate response to years of rage and frustration at the hands of conservative American policymakers such as Ronald Reagan and George H.W. Bush. "Watching network TV in particular," he argues, "was rather like living in a one-party state whose vast propaganda apparatus was ultimately dependent upon the talents of one overworked clerk. Dissenters were allowed a say on discussion programs. But news reports were ideologically uniform." Once the violence erupted following the acquittal of the four police officers, the media shifted from a focus on police brutality to the problem of systemic racism, O'Sullivan claims. He asserts that, rather than report what they were actually seeing in riot footage: "'Rage,' [the reporters] intone, as cheerful looters rush past the camera laughing at their good fortune. 'Protestors,' they explain, as criminal gangs beat up passersby."

Although agreeing that the media failed to accurately report what was happening following the verdict, some take the view that the reporting created racial stereotypes. According to community groups, minority media, and academics who testified at California State Assembly hearings on the causes of the riots, local newspapers and television reporters were so out of touch with the community that they were unprepared for the response following the verdict. According to journalism professor Susan Paterno, this led to racial stereotyping and blatant inaccuracies. For example, one reporter said that the Latino looters looked like illegal aliens. Still another claimed that the destruction was tragic in that recently companies were now willing to reinvest in South Central Los Angeles. In reality, in the ten years prior to the 1992 riots, seventy thousand South Central manufacturing jobs had moved overseas or to Mexico. Indeed, newspaper editor Kenneth Thomas maintains that the media failed to report the riots for what they were: "This is a class issue, not a race issue." When the media showed Korean merchants shooting at looters, Thomas asserts that they "just happened to be Korean. How many blacks get blown away by blacks? That doesn't mean blacks are prejudiced against blacks. [Yet] the mainstream media presented it as though Koreans are trigger-happy."

Some journalists maintain that the images and reporting during the 1992 Los Angeles riots actually fueled the destruction. The coverage so incensed one Korean American journalist that after the riots he left mainstream journalism. Former *Los Angeles Times* reporter John Lee maintains that if the reported incident during the riots was not racialized, it would not be covered. Thus, editors passed over coverage of non-African American and non-Korean disputes. "As the escalation of strong-armed robberies at Korean-owned stores began to correspond with published reports about Black-Korean tension, I realized what was happening was not only very wrong, it was poor journalism. And so after much thought, I decided to leave the *Times*. End of story." In truth, Bob Tur and Marika Gerrard, the journalists who filmed the beating of truck driver Reginald Denny, assert that the filming may have made the criminally minded aware that there were no police presence at the intersection of Florence and Normandie Avenues, the site of the attack on Denny. However, they also remark that the filming let others know that Denny needed help, inspiring his rescuers. Moreover, the footage helped police identify his attackers. For journalists, balancing competing interests when reporting during a crisis poses great challenges. Lee concludes, "Although I've long since tried to come to terms with the riots, a resolution has yet to present itself."

Commentators continue to debate exactly how media images reflect or color what people remember of the

1992 Los Angeles riots. For many, whether the images that frame their perspective reflect what actually happened during the riots is less important than what the events say about racial and ethnic tension in the United States and what America may or may not have learned from the riots. The authors in *Perspectives on Modern World History: The 1992 Los Angeles Riots* tell their stories and share their views on this violent and destructive series of events.

World Map

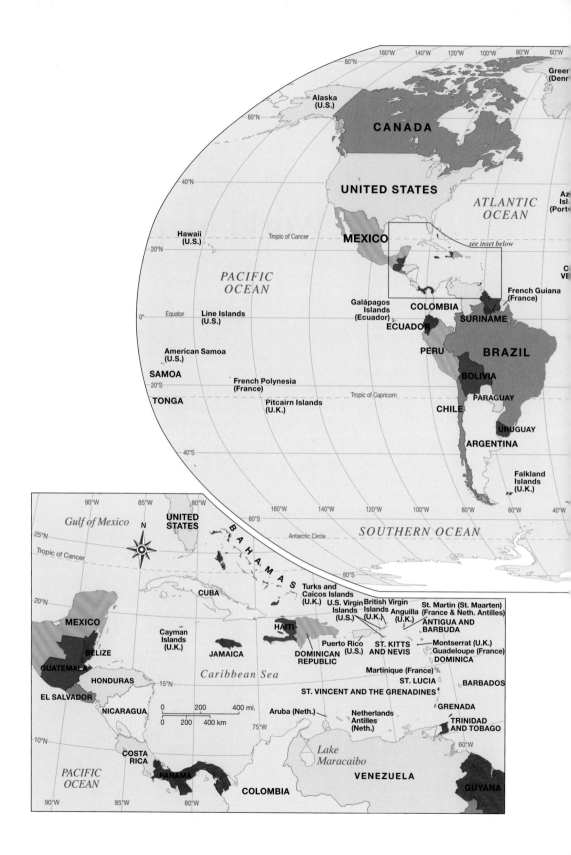

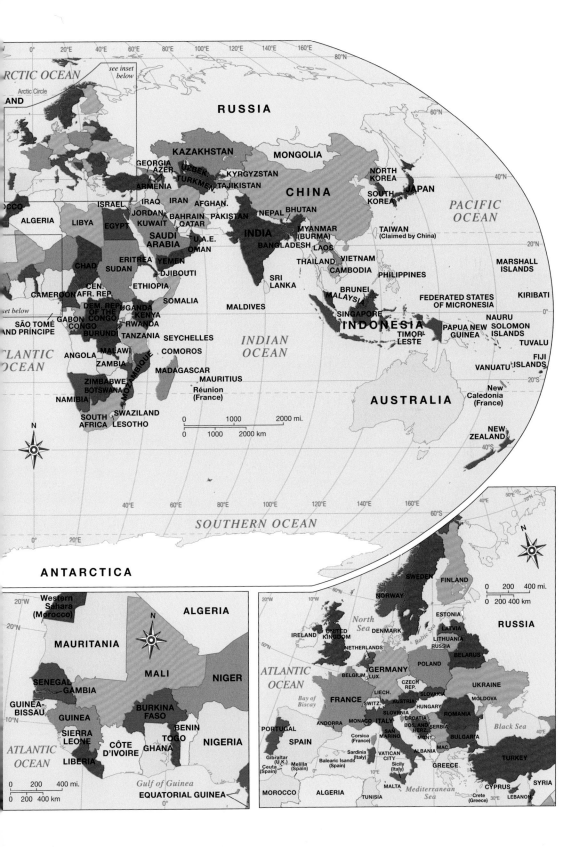

CHAPTER 1

Historical Background on the 1992 Los Angeles Riots

Los Angeles Uprising (1992)

Charles Rosenberg

In the following viewpoint, a historian summarizes the complex events that sparked the 1992 Los Angeles riots and fueled the violence. Many who watched the oft-televised videotape of the 1991 Rodney King beating expected the four Los Angeles Police Department officers charged with excessive force to be convicted. Thus, when a jury acquitted all four officers, outraged Los Angeles citizens immediately began to protest. The reaction turned violent in South Central Los Angeles, fueled by ethnic tension, the presence of gangs, and widespread unemployment. The police were completely unprepared for the response to the verdict. Widespread

Photo on previous page: Fires set by rioters burn residential and commercial buildings in Los Angeles, California, in April 1992. (© Kypros/ **Hulton Archive/Getty Images.**)

SOURCE. Republished with permission of ABC-CLIO, from "Los Angeles Uprising (1992)," *Revolts, Protests, Demonstrations, and Rebellions in American History: An Encyclopedia, Charles Rosenberg,* edited by Steven L. Danver, vol. 3, 2011, pp. 1095–1100; permission conveyed through Copyright Clearance Center, Inc.

looting and arson marked the days that followed. Despite the senseless death and destruction, the riots nevertheless revealed the heroics of those who tried to help. Charles Rosenberg is an independent scholar of history and contributes to several history publications, including *Revolts, Protests, Demonstrations, and Rebellions in American History: An Encyclopedia.*

Two events triggered the combination of uprising, protests, indiscriminate violence, and generalized looting that struck Los Angeles between April 29 and May 4, 1992. One was the beating and arrest of Rodney King on March 2, 1991. The other was the trial of four of the 20 or so police officers present. Like all real-life incidents, the arrest and trial were more complex than any viewpoint in the political debate surrounding them.

King was driving under the influence of alcohol at least 80 miles per hour, ignored direction to pull over, and led police on a chase. Few have questioned that there were grounds for a traffic stop, or an arrest. A portion of the stop was recorded on videotape by a man who lived about 90 feet away. Almost everyone who saw the tape— civilians, news reporters, police supervisors in and out of Los Angeles—found the beating viewed on tape reprehensible and unjustified. The four officers charged with criminal misconduct testified that the tape only showed part of what they had to deal with.

By all accounts, King was intoxicated, but there is little testimony that he was violent. He danced around, rolled on the ground, did not respond quickly to orders. State patrol officer Melanie Singer, who initiated the chase, testified at the trial that she was shocked by the way Los Angeles city officers, after joining the chase when King left the freeway, beat King into submission. Stacey Koon, the L.A. police sergeant who took charge, said he was professionally disgusted that Singer drew her pistol, when initially demanding that King lie down on the ground. Koon considered that dangerous and unnecessary.

The largest number of baton blows directed at King came from Officer Laurence Powell, who at the beginning of his shift had failed a test for proper delivery of power strokes. By all accounts, he did a lot of damage to King without securing compliance. While Powell says he responded in fear for his life when King charged at him, King testified that he ran toward Powell with his hands up, to show he had no gun. Most of the tape showed King lying on the ground, apparently dodging blows from the baton and occasional kicks. King himself testified that he wondered, "What did I do to deserve this?" and that when it ended, he "felt like a crushed can."

All officers denied racial bias in their treatment of King. King's attorney, Steven Lerman, initially agreed, saying the beating was an extreme example of the use of force after a high-speed chase. Later examination of Powell's police communications raised some question. He had described intervention in a large party as "right out of *Gorillas in the Mist*," to which another officer replied "Let me guess who be the parties." Koon, however, was liked and respected by African American officers, and there was no evidence of racial bias by Powell's trainee, Timothy Wind. Theodore Briseno, the fourth officer charged, had been suspended in 1987 for using force on a handcuffed child abuse suspect, but was critical of the treatment of King even before it was known that the beating had been taped. The jury arrived at one conclusion; almost everyone else, on the street or in public office, expected another.

Nobody in Los Angeles on April 29, 1992, was prepared for all four police officers facing criminal charges in the beating of Rodney

> Nobody in Los Angeles on April 29, 1992, was prepared for all four police officers facing criminal charges in the beating of Rodney King to walk out with no convictions.

THE 1992 LOS ANGELES RIOTS: BY THE NUMBERS

9 minutes 22 seconds	Duration of George Holliday video of the Rodney King beating
0	African Americans on the jury in the trial of the LAPD officers accused of assault and use of excessive force in the Rodney King case
7 days	Length of jury deliberation in the same case
30 minutes	Amount of time between the announcement that all four officers had been acquitted and a crowd of 300 gathering outside of the Los Angeles County courthouse
6 days	Duration of riots
At least 53	Deaths
2,383	Injuries
More than 16,000	Riot-related crimes reported
12,111	Arrests
7,000	Fires
$1 billion (estimate)	Value of property damage

King to walk out with no convictions. The police department was not prepared for it; neither were the bitterly divided ethnic communities in Los Angeles, civil rights and community organizations, the news media, the state of California, or the public across the United States. Everyone had seen a videotape of police beating King on March 2, 1991, played on TV over and over, for a year before the trial. Everyone expected at least some officers would be convicted of at least some charges. The trial had been moved to suburban Simi Valley, but even there, many people expected convictions.

When the news came that Koon, Wind, and Briseno had been found not guilty on all charges, while the jury had been unable to agree on a verdict for one charge against Powell, the response was unorganized, spontaneous, and outraged. Initial police response was disorganized and, in many respects, nonexistent. Two immediate centers of loud, angry, but relatively peaceful protests drew ethnically diverse crowds, gathering spontaneously on April 29: the site at Hansen Dam Park where King had been beaten and arrested, and the Parker Center, downtown police headquarters.

Protesters at Parker Center introduced the slogan "No Justice, No Peace" for which the entire uprising is remembered. Eventually, someone set fire to a kiosk, motivating police to move their line pushing protesters away. Some moved west toward City Hall and the Los Angeles Times building, breaking windows along the way; others set fire to palm trees along the Hollywood freeway. The same evening, over 2,000 people came to a protest meeting at First African Methodist Episcopal Church. All these protests were soon submerged in news of more lurid and violent events in South Central, Hoover Connection, Compton, and Pico-Union.

Along Normandie Avenue, honking horns up and down the street, shouting outside a police station, gave rise to incidents of men with baseball bats smashing windows of passing cars, then crowds on corners throwing rocks. A little after 4:00 P.M., at Florence and Dalton, several men walked out of a corner store with bottles of beer, swinging one at the head of the storeowner trying to stop them, remarking, "This is for Rodney King." Responding to reports of motorists attacked and officers needing backup at the corner of Florence and Normandie, 30 to 35 officers faced a rock-throwing crowd of more than

200, when police lieutenant Michael Moulin ordered evacuation of the area. Several officers said afterward that they disagreed with the order.

The police department's Metropolitan division, the usual backup for a situation out of control, had 233 officers, 76 of them off duty at 6:00 P.M. Of the remaining 157, 46 were in the San Fernando Valley, far from the scene, and another 29 were at the Parker Center downtown. This left 82 for deployment in South Central. No contingency plans had been made for any outbreak. Police chief Daryl Gates spent the evening at a fundraiser advocating a "no" vote on Proposition F, a ballot measure to reform the police department. Nobody in any police chain of command took initiative to block off either streets becoming dangerous for motorists or freeway exits; the state highway patrol belatedly blocked some exits.

Outside Los Angeles, the iconic image of the uprising was another videotape: several young men at the corner of Florence and Normandie [avenues], pulling Reginald Denny from the cab of his concrete truck and beating him with fists, kicks, and a cinderblock until he was rescued by four residents in the area. That video was taken from a news helicopter overhead, where Bob and Marika Tur urgently observed that there was no police presence anywhere nearby. Many others pulled out of cars and beaten at the same corner were Asian or Latino, rescued by African American residents of the area. A large portion of those throwing rocks and beating motorists in the area were flashing gang signs. Sixty percent of residents in the area owned their own homes, but some 40,000 teens aged 16–19 were out of school and out of work.

The next three days were not marked by political protest nor acts of rage, but by looting in areas where police

> The iconic image of the uprising was . . . several young men at the corner of Florence and Normandie [Avenues], pulling Reginald Denny from the cab of his concrete truck and beating him.

Amateur video shot by George Holliday (and shown on local TV station KTLA) shows Los Angeles police officers beating Rodney King on March 3, 1991. A year later, the acquittal in the criminal case against the officers sparked protests, riots, violence, and looting. (© Charles Steiner/Image Works/ Time Life Pictures/Getty Images.)

presence had been withdrawn or was stretched thin. More than half the residents in the affected areas were Latino, as were a majority of the looters; most of those young single men only recently arrived in the city. Rodney King was not the issue after the first hours on April 29; a white and a Latino looter, attempting to rob a grocery store, told the African American owner, "F—Rodney King." The owner, with a .357 Magnum, wounded the white robber, who was carrying a rifle.

A few business owners defended their premises. Richard Ree, owner of California Market, armed family and employees and held off looters on April 30. Art Washington, who had a pest control business on Western Avenue at 20th Street, held off would-be looters, shouting "I *worked* for that. Don't burn down none of my business. I worked too *hard* for this! You call this black power?" Looters did invade and torch the Watts Labor Community Action Center, built after the 1965 Watts riots.

Four thousand California National Guard troops, 4,500 federal troops, including 1,500 marines, and 1,000 federal law enforcement officers, were sent into Los Angeles to restore a semblance of peace. A curfew imposed on May 1 was lifted the night of May 4. There were 54 confirmed deaths—26 African American, 14 Latino, nine white, and two Asian, with three bodies too badly burned for identification. At least 2,328 were treated for injuries, 862 structures damaged by fire, with a total of $900 million in property damage.

> There were 54 confirmed deaths —26 African American, 14 Latino, nine white, and two Asian, with three bodies too badly burned for identification.

Among the first three killed were Dwight (Fishman) Taylor, an African American fish cutter; Matthew Haines, a white mechanic; and Elbert Wilkins, a black stereo shop owner. Taylor was shot by unknown assailants while walking to a store near his job at All Seas Fish Market. Wilkins was hit by bullets from a passing car, talking to friends near his business. Haines was on his way to rescue an African American family friend who worried about violence in her neighborhood, when he was dragged off his motorcycle and shot at point-blank range by a mob in Long Beach. Haines's father told a Los Angeles TV station "if this had been a declared war, my son would have signed up" on the same side as the people who shot him.

One of the jurors in the trial of the police officers said, "I can't believe all this is a reaction to what we did." Mayor Tom Bradley announced, with evident anger, "Today, the jury told the world that what we all saw with our own eyes was not a crime." The jury had spent the trial in a quiet courtroom, pouring over details of each police officer's testimony. To most people on the street, that was not the point. Everyone in the poorer areas of the city knew of someone mistreated by police, from outright shooting to being handled roughly after a traffic stop. So did many African Americans from prosperous neighborhoods, and more than a few Latinos. Generally, charges against officers involved had been dismissed for lack of convincing evidence, while the city paid between $3.7 million and $13 million a year in civil damages. This time, the police had been caught on tape; everyone expected that for once, they would be convicted.

The death of Latasha Harlins, a high school student with ambitions to become a prosecuting attorney, added to the sense of injustice and futility. She had been shot in the back of the head by the checkout clerk in a corner store, where the security camera showed that Soon Ja Du initiated a confrontation, mistakenly thinking Harlins intended to steal a bottle of orange juice. Harlins had walked away from the conflict, without the orange juice, when she was shot. A jury convicted Du of voluntary manslaughter, but on November 11, 1991, Judge Joyce Ann Karlin imposed five years probation, suggesting that Du did not mean to kill Harlins, contradicting the jury's verdict.

Dallas, Texas, police chief William Rathburn, a former LA assistant chief, had publicly called the beating of King "gross criminal misconduct." LAPD officer Tom Sullivan said "This isn't just a case of excessive force. It's a case of mass stupidity." By March 10, 1992, 86 percent of those contacted for a *Los Angeles Times* poll had seen the tape, and 92 percent thought excessive force had been used. In mid-April, 81 percent in another survey believed the four officers to be guilty of criminal assault. Since jury selection generally excludes anyone with a well-formed opinion on guilt or innocence, the jury would inevitably have been drawn from the small minority disposed to think the police may have acted appropriately.

A Local Newspaper Reports Citizen Reactions in Riot-Torn South Los Angeles

Jonathan Peterson and Hector Tobar

On May 1, 1992, the third day of the Los Angeles riots, *Los Angeles Times* staff writers ventured into the streets to talk to people living in South Central Los Angeles as it still burned. In the following viewpoint, interviewees say the loss of life and property makes life even more difficult in neighborhoods with few banks or stores. Without cars, they will have to travel long distances by bus to shop for necessities. One black business owner in a community where black-owned businesses are rare reveals that tension increased with the influx of Korean-American merchants. Nevertheless, the self-inflicted destruction to others seems senseless. The people of the community seem divided on the violence and looting—some saying that the response was, if not justified, understandable. Left with conflicting views and images, the authors conclude that the future for these Los Angeles residents remains unclear. Jonathan Peterson and Hector Tobar both won a Pulitzer Prize as part of the *Los Angeles Times* team covering the riots.

I n a smoky parking lot in South Los Angeles, Ruby Galude, 55, stared in disbelief at the wreckage of her local grocery store. "I'm a diabetic. This is where I get all my juices and foods," she said, peering at shards of glass and soaked debris. "What am I going to do now?"

A few miles away, Paul C. Hudson arrived at his family-run savings and loan, a community fixture since 1947 in a neighborhood that has a grave shortage of banks. On Wednesday night it burned down. "Just the exterior wall was left standing," he said.

Anthony Wright and his wife, Jaye, meanwhile, sat in lawn chairs, as radio news blared from their pickup truck. Just a few blocks away, hundreds of people were on a looting rampage on Vermont Avenue.

Hard times fuel the fury, said Jaye Wright, a teacher's aide. "It's not a recession for minority communities. It's a depression."

Long before this week's spasm of destruction, daily life in parts of South Los Angeles was grueling in ways much different from elsewhere in the city. In ordinary, mundane ways—from a shortage of grocery stores and credit at normal interest rates to a scarcity of jobs and the more publicized ills of crime and drugs—it was often hard to get through a typical day.

Now, the rising toll in human life, torched businesses and destroyed property are adding insult to an already dangerous, frustrating existence.

Voices of Hope and Disappointment

On Thursday, [April 30, 1992] some residents spoke in determined voices about getting on with the job of

Residents of South Central Los Angeles wait for a bus in front of shops damaged during the 1992 riots. The destruction caused by the riots created additional hardships for the predominantly poor people who lived in riot-torn areas. (© Marmaduke St. John/Alamy.)

rebuilding their community. There were brave pronouncements of commitment to the future; promises that shellshocked South Los Angeles would pick itself up and, with the aid of new investment, move forward after the rioting subsides.

"We have an obligation to reopen," said Hudson, president of Broadway Federal Savings and Loan, whose green, two-story headquarters on 45th Street survived the Watts riots but not the current mayhem.

However, there were other voices as well—voices of profound disappointment in this country, angry accusations that years of economic injustice and neglect set the stage for violence. And behind the veil of smoke and chaos, a pessimism also seemed to rise—a pessimism that tomorrow might not be better than today, after all.

Baciliso Merino, a short, muscular construction worker, said that life in the city has turned out far worse than he ever dreamed when he brought his family to South Los Angeles from central Mexico a year ago. Wednesday night, he had to climb to the roof of his yellow stucco home to hose down embers that were landing from nearby fires.

But even in normal times, he worries about drive-by shootings and other crime. The unsettling roar of police helicopters is common background noise; police routinely close off streets in pursuit of drug dealers, leaving law-abiding residents marooned in the neighborhood.

America has turned out like "a golden cage," he said, quoting a Mexican song, as black ribbons of smoke rose to the north, south and east of his home near Slauson. "You expect to find so much wealth, but instead you find a prison."

A Commercially Deprived Community

In part, the deprivation is in everyday commercial life, where people often have to pay higher prices with fewer choices, where residents who want to cash checks sometimes wait in endless lines more reminiscent of Moscow than Los Angeles.

> "Dazed residents worried that life in the worst neighborhoods will become even more thankless. . . .

Since the days of the Watts riots, most major supermarket chains have cut back their stores in South Los Angeles. Other retailers are wary of settling there altogether. On Thursday, Thrifty Drug—which lost four outlets during the 1965 Watts riots—reported that it has lost three stores this week, shut down 11, and may not rebuild those that are destroyed.

Dazed residents worried that life in the worst neighborhoods will become even more thankless, with the help of self-inflicted wounds. People "won't have anywhere to eat. They won't have anywhere to buy gas. They won't have anywhere to buy groceries," said Jacquie Wade, who had ventured into a strife-torn neighborhood to see if her church was still standing. It was.

She was in a small shopping center near Figueroa Street, where other structures suffered a different fate. A public library and hamburger stand had been transformed to smoldering rubble.

The frustrations are also a product of limited jobs. Famous manufacturers, such as General Motors, Goodyear, Firestone and Bethlehem Steel, all used to provide South Los Angeles residents the chance for a living wage and upward mobility—including those without education.

By the 1980s, most such jobs vanished, a result of declining U.S. competitiveness. In the ashes, residents were forced into a lower-wage economy of light industry, welding shops, furniture makers, garment factories, fast-food restaurants and other employers.

But even those employers are taking a pounding in the recent bedlam, with a further loss to the community.

"You're talking about janitorial-maintenance companies, clothing stores, restaurants, cleaners," said Gene Hale, chairman of the African-American Chamber of Commerce. "You can go across the board—these are little shopping centers, with businesses nailed together. One fire will get them all."

A Profound Population Change Brings Tension

Much of the new business reflects profound population change, which has brought new tensions: As recently as 10 years ago, most of the population was African-American; since then, an influx of Korean-American merchants and Latino residents has turned South Los Angeles into a melting pot.

But the black residents have long complained that some of their newer neighbors, who often own small shops, do not treat them with respect.

"It's sad," said Moddie V. Wilson III, who posted hastily scribbled signs on the front windows of his hardware store at Crenshaw and 43rd Place, saying "Black-Owned Business," to ward off potential looters.

"Black people are disenfranchised in this community. We don't have many stores, but some had started to come back. Now I don't know. It's gotten beyond Rodney King. Rodney King was just the straw that broke the camel's back."

One looter, casually walking along Western Avenue with a brand-new stereo speaker, voiced the outrage of many black residents toward some of the immigrant merchants: "These businesses (we) burned down don't care about us," he said. He further cited the case of Latasha Harlins, the 15-year-old high school student who was shot to death by a Korean storekeeper. The storekeeper, convicted of voluntary manslaughter, was placed on probation. "They just charge high prices and take our money. Now we are taking some back."

Property seemed to have special symbolism to the street vandals. While residents raised their fists at police cars and cried, "No justice! No peace!" it was retailers, factories and other enterprises that received the brunt of a rage that some residents and community experts say stems from a painful economic isolation.

> While residents raised their fists at police cars and cried, "No justice! No peace!" it was retailers, factories and other enterprises that received the brunt of [the] rage.

While not condoning lawlessness, some community leaders sought at least to offer some insight into the violence. Carl Dickerson, president of the Black Business Assn. of Los Angeles, spoke of the perceived analogy between injustice in the courthouse and injustice in the job market.

The outpouring of rage, he maintained, comes in part because many people associate the verdict in the King case with "economic injustice" in their own lives.

"Reacting to this miscarriage of justice . . . prompts people to conclude that the system has also treated them unfairly," Dickerson said. "They should have jobs and opportunities, but they don't. The recession has resulted in a reduction of jobs, mergers have led to job loss, the aerospace industry is losing jobs and there is a flight of industry from California."

Businesses Have Left the Community

With fewer than 35 major supermarkets and 20 banks and thrifts serving a 35-square-mile area of more than half a million people, South Los Angeles has grown a world apart from the traditional wheels of commerce as businesses have fled.

Today, in some sections of South Los Angeles, the nearest full-service grocery stores are often at least two bus rides away and neighborhood mom-and-pop stores sometimes charge as much as 30% more than bigger retailers.

Meanwhile, there are so few banks and thrifts that residents routinely stand in lines for hours to make a deposit or cash a check. In fact, financial institutions are so scarce, that in some areas of South Los Angeles armored trucks rumble to job sites on paydays to cash checks for workers.

"I don't think black people really want to put anybody out of business," said Patsy Brown, a well-known Crenshaw-area businesswoman who kept her Papa's Grocery store on Vernon and Van Ness open all day Thursday amid the raging fires and looting in nearby blocks.

"But they are angry that they have no choice (of merchants) in their community. People have supported me

Rodney King's Plea for Peace

Riots broke out in Los Angeles, California, after the acquittal of four Los Angeles police officers for the beating of motorist Rodney King. King's beating at the hands of the police, caught on videotape, had outraged the nation, and the acquittal of the officers involved was seen by many as the result of a racist and corrupt legal system. In an attempt to quell the violence in Los Angeles, King made this plea for peace:

People, I just want to say, can we all get along? Can we get along? Can we stop making it horrible for older people and the kids?

I mean, we've got enough smog here in Los Angeles, let alone to deal with setting these fires and things. It's just not right; it's not right. And it's not going to change anything. We'll get our justice. They've won the battle, but they haven't won the war. We'll have our day in court, and that's all we want.

I'm neutral. I love everybody. I love people of color. You know, I'm not like they're making me out to be. We've got to quit. We've got to quit. After all, I mean, I can understand the first upset, for the first two hours after the verdict. But to go on—to keep going on like this and to see this security guard shot on the ground, it's just not right. It's just not right because those people will never go home to their families again.

I mean, please, we can get along here. We can all get along. We've just got to. I mean, we're all stuck here for a while. Let's try to work it out. Let's try to beat it. Let's try to work it out.

SOURCE. *"Rodney G. King's Statement, May 1, 1992,"* Discovering U.S. History. *Detroit: Gale, 2003.*

not because I'm black, but because I give good service to them. A lot of these other stores can't [make that claim]," Brown said.

Near a corner mini-mall on Figueroa Street, two young men discussed the eerie drama unfolding before their eyes, as the remnants of a store, now unrecognizable, smoldered. Firefighters continued to put out the embers.

Alex Zendejas, 18, said he expected damaged or looted businesses to be reopened. However, he expressed some regret about certain short-term economic losses resulting from the disturbances.

Messing Up the Neighborhood

"Maybe people should have taken their protest to some other neighborhoods," he said.

His friend, Sadi Dukes, 17, agreed. "I'd rather see this happening in Pasadena or Simi Valley," he said. "I don't think people should mess up their own neighborhood."

> "I'd rather see this happening in Pasadena or Simi Valley. . . . I don't think people should mess up their own neighborhood."

Many of the looters, Zendejas added, "have nothing to lose and something to gain."

Other witnesses were outraged, and drew a clear connection between the wanton vandalism and quality of life in the coming days. For example, William Small talked with other neighborhood residents as looters hauled goods from Car Sound, a car stereo retailer on Vermont near 25th Street.

"These looters may not realize it, but this is criminal activity," Small said. "If they're caught and put in jail, they will understand just how criminal this is."

Small said many business owners with riot-related losses have no insurance and will not reopen their enterprises.

"People will have to leave the area just to shop," he said. "I don't have a car. That means I'll have to take a bus to get what I need."

Amid the destruction, some business leaders vowed to rebuild the community, and there were countless acts of heroism and decency. But on the day that South Los Angeles continued to burn, the lasting image was far more dark and bewildering.

At the corner of 43rd Place and Crenshaw, more than a dozen laughing and animated patrons packed the tiny

Crenshaw Cafe's outdoor tables, sipping coffee and dining on a hearty breakfast of pancakes and eggs. Across the street a ferocious fire was blazing, sending a trail of destruction through a manicure shop and the Muslim Community Center.

The US President Condemns Los Angeles Rioters

George H.W. Bush

Two days after violence erupted in Los Angeles in April 1992, President George H.W. Bush delivered the following speech from the Oval Office. It was broadcast nationwide on radio and television. Bush advises the American people of his plan to send National Guardsmen and federal troops to the embattled city. The president tells the American people that he too was stunned by the Rodney King beating verdict and has therefore directed the Justice Department to pursue its own investigation. Despite outrage over injustice, Bush argues that nothing justifies the acts of violence and destruction Americans have witnessed in Los Angeles. He emphasizes that wanton violence is not about civil right but mob brutality. Despite the horrific events of the preceding days, Bush acknowledges that some citizens, regardless of race, came to the aid of riot victims. Bush concludes by asking Americans to work toward understanding and tolerance.

SOURCE. George H.W. Bush, "Address to the Nation on the Civil Disturbances in Los Angeles, California," *Weekly Compilation of Presidential Documents,* vol. 28, no. 18, May 4, 1992, p. 751. Office of the Federal Register.

Tonight [May 1, 1992] I want to talk to you about violence in our cities and justice for our citizens, two big issues that have collided on the streets of Los Angeles. First, an update on where matters stand in Los Angeles.

Fifteen minutes ago I talked to California's Governor Pete Wilson and Los Angeles Mayor Tom Bradley. They told me that last night was better than the night before; today, calmer than yesterday. But there were still incidents of random terror and lawlessness this afternoon.

In the wake of the first night's violence, I spoke directly to both Governor Wilson and Mayor Bradley to assess the situation and to offer assistance. There are two very different issues at hand. One is the urgent need to restore order. What followed Wednesday's jury verdict in the Rodney King case was a tragic series of events for the city of Los Angeles: Nearly 4,000 fires, staggering property damage, hundreds of injuries, and the senseless deaths of over 30 people.

Restoring Order

To restore order right now, there are 3,000 National Guardsmen on duty in the city of Los Angeles. Another 2,200 stand ready to provide immediate support. To supplement this effort I've taken several additional actions. First, this morning I've ordered the Justice Department to dispatch 1,000 Federal riot-trained law enforcement officials to help restore order in Los Angeles beginning tonight. These officials include FBI SWAT teams, special riot control units of the U.S. Marshals Service, the border patrol, and other Federal law enforcement agencies. Second, another 1,000 Federal law enforcement officials are on standby alert, should they be needed. Third, early today I directed 3,000 members of the 7th Infantry and 1,500 marines to stand by at El Toro Air Station, California. Tonight,

The Christopher Commission and the Civil Rights Trial

In the riot's aftermath, criticism of the Los Angeles police, which had escalated after the [Rodney] King beating, grew stronger. Many believed that the longtime police chief, Daryl F. Gates, had not sufficiently prepared for the possibility of civil unrest and had made poor decisions in the first hours of the riots. The view that Gates should be replaced because of the brutality charges, coupled with the determination by an independent commission headed by Warren G. Christopher (a distinguished attorney who served in the State Department during the Carter administration), placed increasing pressure on the police chief. Gates finally resigned in late June 1992.

In August 1992 a federal grand jury indicted the four officers [Stacey C. Koon, Laurence M. Powell, Timothy E. Wind, and Theodore J. Briseno] for violating King's civil rights. Koon was charged with depriving King of due process of law by failing to restrain the other officers. The other three officers were charged with violating King's right against unreasonable search and seizure because they had used unreasonable force during the arrest.

At the federal trial, which was held in Los Angeles, the jury was more racially diverse than the one at Simi Valley: Two jury members were black, one was Hispanic, and the rest were white. This time King testified about the beating and charged that the officers had used racial epithets. Observers agreed that he was an effective witness. The videotape again was the central piece of evidence for both sides. On April 17, 1993, the jury convicted officers Koon and Powell of violating King's civil rights but acquitted Wind and Briseno. Koon and Powell were sentenced to two and a half years in prison.

SOURCE. *"King, Rodney G.," in Donna Batten, ed.,* Gale Encyclopedia of American Law, *third edition, vol. 6. Detroit: Gale, 2011, p. 167.*

at the request of the Governor and the mayor, I have committed these troops to help restore order. I'm also federalizing the National Guard, and I'm instructing General Colin Powell to place all those troops under a central command.

What we saw last night and the night before in Los Angeles is not about civil rights. It's not about the great cause of equality that all Americans must uphold. It's not a message of protest. It's been the brutality of a mob, pure and simple. And let me assure you: I will use whatever force is necessary to restore order. What is going on in L.A. must and will stop. As your President I guarantee you this violence will end.

> What we saw last night and the night before in Los Angeles is not about civil rights. . . . It's been the brutality of a mob, pure and simple.

A Surprising Verdict

Now let's talk about the beating of Rodney King, because beyond the urgent need to restore order is the second issue, the question of justice: Whether Rodney King's Federal civil rights were violated. What you saw and what I saw on the TV video was revolting. I felt anger. I felt pain. I thought: How can I explain this to my grandchildren?

Civil rights leaders and just plain citizens fearful of, and sometimes victimized by, police brutality were deeply hurt. And I know good and decent policemen who were equally appalled.

I spoke this morning to many leaders of the civil rights community. And they saw the video, as we all did. For 14 months they waited patiently, hopefully. They waited for the system to work. And when the verdict came in, they felt betrayed. Viewed from outside the trial, it was hard to understand how the verdict could possibly square with the video. Those civil rights leaders with whom I met were stunned, and so was I and so was Barbara and so were my kids.

Ensuring That Justice Is Served

But the verdict Wednesday was not the end of the process. The Department of Justice had started its own investigation immediately after the Rodney King incident and was monitoring the State investigation and trial. And so let me tell you what actions we are taking on the Federal level to ensure that justice is served.

Within one hour of the verdict, I directed the Justice Department to move into high gear on its own independent criminal investigation into the case. And next, on Thursday, five Federal prosecutors were on their way to Los Angeles. Our Justice Department has consistently demonstrated its ability to investigate fully a matter like this.

Since 1988, the Justice Department has successfully prosecuted over 100 law enforcement officials for excessive violence. I am confident that in this case, the Department of Justice will act as it should. Federal grand jury action is underway today in Los Angeles. Subpoenas are being issued. Evidence is being reviewed. The Federal effort in this case will be expeditious, and it will be fair. It will not be driven by mob violence but by respect for due process and the rule of law.

We owe it to all Americans who put their faith in the law to see that justice is served. But as we move forward on this or any other case, we must remember the fundamental tenet of our legal system. Every American, whether accused or accuser, is entitled to protection of his or her rights.

In this highly controversial court case, a verdict was handed down by a California jury. To Americans of all races who were shocked by the verdict, let me say this: You must understand that our system of justice provides for the peaceful, orderly means of addressing this frustration.

> " In a civilized society, there can be no excuses, no excuse for the murders, arson, theft, and vandalism that have terrorized the law-abiding citizens of Los Angeles. "

We must respect the process of law whether or not we agree with the outcome. There's a difference between frustration with the law and direct assaults upon our legal system.

In a civilized society, there can be no excuse, no excuse for the murder, arson, theft, and vandalism that have terrorized the law-abiding citizens of Los Angeles. Mayor Bradley, just a few minutes ago, mentioned to me his particular concern, among others, regarding the safety of the Korean community. My heart goes out to them and all others who have suffered losses.

The wanton destruction of life and property is not a legitimate expression of outrage with injustice. It is itself injustice. And no rationalization, no matter how heart-felt, no matter how eloquent, can make it otherwise.

Viewing the Unforgettable Images

Television has become a medium that often brings us together. But its vivid display of Rodney King's beating shocked us. The America it has shown us on our screens these last 48 hours has appalled us. None of this is what we wish to think of as American. It's as if we were looking in a mirror that distorted our better selves and turned us ugly. We cannot let that happen. We cannot do that to ourselves.

We've seen images in the last 48 hours that we will never forget. Some were horrifying almost beyond belief. But there were other acts, small but significant acts in all this ugliness that give us hope. I'm one who respects our police. They keep the peace. They face danger every day. They help kids. They don't make a lot of money, but they care about their communities and their country. Thousands of police officers and firefighters are risking their lives right now on the streets of L.A., and they deserve our support. Then there are the people who have spent each night not in the streets but in the churches of Los Angeles, praying that man's gentler instincts be revealed in the hearts of people driven by hate. And finally, there were the citizens who showed great personal responsibility, who ignored the mob, who at great personal danger helped the victims of violence, regardless of race.

Among the many stories I've seen and heard about these past few days, one sticks in my mind, the story of one savagely beaten white truck driver, alive tonight because four strangers, four black strangers, came to his aid. Two were men who had been watching television and saw the beating as it was happening, and came out into the street to help; another was a woman on her way home from work; and the fourth, a young man whose name we may never know. The injured driver was able to get behind the wheel of his truck and tried to drive away. But his eyes were swollen shut. The woman asked him if he could see. He answered, "No." She said, "Well, then I will be your eyes." Together, those four people braved the mob and drove that truck driver to the hospital. He's alive today only because they stepped in to help.

Rebuilding Hope

It is for every one of them that we must rebuild the community of Los Angeles, for these four people and the others like them who in the midst of this nightmare acted with simple human decency.

> We must keep on working to create a climate of understanding and tolerance, a climate that refuses to accept racism, bigotry, anti-Semitism, and hate of any kind, anytime, anywhere.

We must understand that no one in Los Angeles or any other city has rendered a verdict on America. If we are to remain the most vibrant and hopeful Nation on Earth we must allow our diversity to bring us together, not drive us apart. This must be the rallying cry of good and decent people.

For their sake, for all our sakes, we must build a future where, in every city across this country, empty rage

gives way to hope, where poverty and despair give way to opportunity. After peace is restored to Los Angeles, we must then turn again to the underlying causes of such tragic events. We must keep on working to create a climate of understanding and tolerance, a climate that refuses to accept racism, bigotry, anti-Semitism, and hate of any kind, anytime, anywhere.

Tonight, I ask all Americans to lend their hearts, their voices, and their prayers to the healing of hatred. As President, I took an oath to preserve, protect, and defend the Constitution, an oath that requires every President to establish justice and ensure domestic tranquility. That duty is foremost in my mind tonight.

A pair of national guardsmen patrol a riot-torn Los Angeles street on April 30, 1992. US president George H.W. Bush sent thirty thousand troops to the area to help restore order. (© Hal Garb/AFP/Getty Images.)

Let me say to the people saddened by the spectacle of the past few days, to the good people of Los Angeles, caught at the center of this senseless suffering: The violence will end. Justice will be served. Hope will return.

Thank you, and may God bless the United States of America.

A Rap Artist Condones the Los Angeles Riots as a Racial Rebellion

David Mills

In the following viewpoint, a journalist recounts rap artist Sister Souljah's defense of the Los Angeles riots. In television news and talk show interviews, Souljah maintains that riots were a justified form of rebellion against white oppression. That the oppressive conditions that lead black people to kill other black people would lead to violence against whites should not surprise white Americans, she claims. The author suggests that those who question whether Souljah's view of the violence is widespread should consider that rap music reflects the views of millions. When asked if she thought the lives of the riot victims did not matter, Souljah responds that if the deaths of black people do not matter, why it should matter that white people die. In the eyes of Souljah, revenge against the harm done in the name of white supremacy is justified against all whites. David Mills was a television writer and journalist who wrote for the *Washington Post,* the *Washington Times,* and the *Wall Street Journal.*

> Souljah was not born to make white people feel comfortable. I am African first. I am black first. I want what's good for me and my people first. And if my survival means your total destruction, then so be it. You built this wicked system. They say two wrongs don't make it right, but it damn sure makes it even.
>
> —Sister Souljah, from the song "The
> Hate That Hate Produced," 1992.

After the Rodney King verdict and its fiery aftermath, Sister Souljah, a rapper and orator, appeared on NBC's *Sunday Today* with Sen. Bill Bradley (D-N.J.) and Rep. Charles Rangel (D-N.Y.). And she sat alongside black professors from Yale and Columbia on Bill Moyers's PBS series *Listening to America.*

A Chilling Wake-Up Call

She calmly explained that African Americans are "at war," and that the explosion in Los Angeles was "revenge" against a system of white oppression.

But during an interview in Washington last week [May 1992], Souljah's empathy for the rioters reached a chilling extreme. Forget the statistics emerging on the racial variety of looters and people who died. Forget the economic motives of those who plundered stores. To Souljah, this was a black-on-white "rebellion," plain and simple and righteous.

> I mean, if black people kill black people every day, why not have a week and kill white people? You understand what I'm saying? In other words, white people, this government and that mayor were well aware of the fact

that black people were dying every day in Los Angeles under gang violence. So if you're a gang member and you would normally be killing somebody, why not kill a white person? Do you think that somebody thinks that white people are better, or above dying, when they would kill their own kind?

As she said on *Sunday Today*: "Unfortunately for white people, they think it's all right for our children to die, for our men to be in prison, and not theirs."

Sister Souljah will be back on "Today" this morning, live from Burbank. Consider it a wake-up call.

Whose analysis of the violence in Los Angeles, in the months and years to come, will matter more? The conservative pundit's, placing blame squarely on young criminals who "terrorized" a city? The liberal politician's, bemoaning poverty and the neglect of our cities? Or the radical rapper's, asserting that white people and Korean merchants had it coming?

Ask the kids who watch MTV.

The Political Power of Rap

The King verdict and its backlash have shown America the power of hip-hop music as a political medium. Television coverage of the crisis confirmed, as never before, the status of hard-edged rappers as spokesmen for the black lower class, delegates of America's angry youth. Opinion-makers. Leaders.

"Whoever wants to speak to young people will have to come through the corridor of hip-hop," says Sister Souljah, whose debut album, *360 Degrees of Power*, came out last month. Born Lisa Williamson twentysomething years ago, she was a New York community activist

> Television coverage of the [Los Angeles] crisis confirmed, as never before, the status of hard-edged rappers as spokesmen for the black lower class, delegates of America's angry youth.

and established public speaker before launching her rap career under the auspices of Public Enemy, standard-bearers of hip-hop's militant wing. As rap has grown in popularity among black and white listeners, offering everything from cute kids (Kris Kross) to professing Christians (Hammer) to raunchy comedians (2 Live Crew), political rappers have come to be considered its conscience.

"When it was really understood that rap music makes millions of dollars, and that rap artists represent the voices of millions of young people," Souljah says, "I think that's when all the institutions of America came to their senses about having to involve a rap artist in their analysis. [With] a rebellion carried out primarily by African youth, how could you ignore African youth? It would be impossible. Not if you were a serious journalist."

Bill Moyers showed a clip from one of Souljah's fulminating videos—The time for scared, lip-trembling, word-changing, self-denying, compromising, knee-shaking black people is over!—then asked her, "How would you like me—I'm white—to interpret your work?"

"Well," she responded politely, a bit of the Bronx in her voice, "I don't make my work for you to interpret it. I make it for black young people so that they can understand that we are at war, that we have to be strong-minded, that we have to be productive, that we have to be unafraid of expressing ourselves and getting what we want in this society."

Shattering Boundaries

Rappers like Sister Souljah are shattering the boundaries between performer and audience, and between entertainment and politics. When a jury acquitted the four Los Angeles policemen who'd beaten Rodney King, X-Clan, a Brooklyn-based activist rap group, was performing at San Francisco State University. The rappers got the news, stopped the show, then led an impromptu

Sister Souljah, an outspoken defender of the rioters in Los Angeles, speaks at a press conference in New York City in June 1992. (© **AP Photo/Alex Brandon.**)

march of about 200 people, chanting "Whose streets? Our streets!" and "[Expletive] the police!"

Which echoes N.W.A.'s infamous revenge fantasy "[Expletive] tha Police," a dream of "a bloodbath of cops dying in L.A." That song, denounced by the Fraternal Order of Police, concludes with the rappers sitting in judgment of a white officer: "The jury has found you guilty of being a redneck, white-bread [expletive expletive]." And the cop pleads, "I want justice! I want justice!" That came out in 1988.

Two members of N.W.A. were interviewed by "MTV News" . . . when the burning and looting got started in south-central. And appearing live on MTV was Chuck D of Public Enemy, whose words "fight the power" reverberate on the soundtrack of Spike Lee's *Do the Right Thing* while the white-owned pizzeria burns to the ground. That came out in 1989.

And Spike Lee begat L.A.'s John Singleton, whose hit film *Boyz n the Hood* took its name from an old N.W.A. song. That movie launched the acting career of ex-N.W.A. member Ice Cube, who provided a new rap for the album *How to Survive in South Central*, yet another piece of ironic foreshadowing. Be alert, stay calm, as you enter the concrete Vietnam. . . . That came out last year [1991].

As did Ice Cube's warning to Korean merchants: Pay respect to the black fist, or we'll burn your store right down to a crisp. That's from his million-selling album, *Death Certificate.*

Entertainment as politics? Politics as entertainment?

A New Media Age

On *The Arsenio Hall Show* last Thursday night, while Johnny Carson and Buddy Hackett were laughing it up in another universe, rapper KRS-One was committing "lyrical terrorism," unleashing brand-new rhymes:

> Now I'm hardcore, walking on the ave, Watching white people look at me then walk fast, After beating us, raping us and robbing us. Four hundred years of that's what's inside of us. Take a look at me now, I'm really your creation. . . .

Even ABC's *Nightline* felt the funk. On May 4, Ted Koppel's extraordinary open-air conversation with L.A. gang members ended with one of them looking into the camera and rapping over a hard beat:

> When you're living in poverty, crazy you gotta be, 'Cause ain't nobody out here looking out for me but me. . . .

This is a new media age. Top 40 radio is dead, and "[Expletive] tha Police" is in the American consciousness. Carson is history, and KRS-One is in America's bedrooms requesting "amnesty" for 13,000 (presumably black) prisoners in Los Angeles. Daily newspapers are folding, and in record stores across America you'll find Ice Cube's news-pegged commentaries, such as this from a duet with Sister Souljah: "You teach freedom of speech, as long as black men don't say Howard Beach, Rodney King or Bensonhurst. Tawana and Tasha, we ain't forgot ya,"[1]

> The [King beating] video images were news, and they were evidence, but they also became a unit of language for hip-hop artists.

Remember too: Everything that has happened in Los Angeles since the King beating is due to a camcorder. The video images were news, and they were evidence, but they also became a unit of language for hip-hop artists. They were spliced into a video for the group B.W.P., and reenacted in a video for Public Enemy. Just as electronic images of the riot/rebellion are bound to show up in rap videos too.

CNN today, MTV tomorrow. At this rate, not only will the revolution be televised, it'll be on pay-per-view. With lots of rap stars.

An Uncompromising Voice

Sister Souljah was sitting in the Capital Hilton lounge pantomiming her "dramatic" stage persona for the benefit of a photographer. Scrunched brow, out-thrust fist, round hot eyes, lips moving staccato.

A finely dressed, middle-aged white woman, sitting nearby with her spoon in some ice cream, stared oddly at the young black woman, then smiled when caught by the eyes of a third party.

Souljah was in Washington last Tuesday to tape an appearance on Black Entertainment Television. This

Sunday she'll be here again, as the keynote speaker at the Malcolm X Day Celebration in Anacostia Park. (X-Clan will be there too, performing.) What she thinks matters.

And the interview at the Hilton may foretell how the militant wing of the hip-hop movement deals with the L.A. crisis in its art. In one sense, Souljah is emblematic of rap-as-politics. Her *360 Degrees of Power* contains probably the most fervid denunciations of white people ever marketed by a major label. (She's signed to Epic Records, which is owned by Sony. How's that for blacks, whites and Asians working together?)

But *360 Degrees* is off to a slow start in the marketplace, and some observers say hip-hop fans consider it too shrill, even though Souljah is a respected voice. "She's not afraid to take a stand," says James Bernard, senior editor of the *Source,* a magazine of "hip-hop culture and politics." "She's one of those uncompromising voices."

But "I'm not sure what Sister Souljah adds to the music, in a musical sense," he says. "When she rhymes, people don't say, 'My God, that's the most incredible line I ever heard in my life.'"

"She kind of screams it out. That's her whole delivery," says Havelock Nelson, rap columnist for *Billboard* magazine. "When I see her speak, I feel the passion and I become moved. You can feel the pain, the anger, whatever she's trying to put across. But I don't think it transfers to the record. I don't think the people want to hear the same lecture in the middle of a jam. A lot of people aren't giving her their ear."

An Unusual Victory

Ironic, then, that Souljah declares on her album: "America is always trying to strangle and silence black people." How does that jibe with her own status as a blossoming media star? Her place in Bill Moyers's Rolodex?

"There's a difference," she said. "I don't evaluate the world solely on my own individual accomplishments, because I recognize that I'm an unusual victory [under] this system of oppression. Usually this system is successful in crushing the spirit, the mind and the hearts of young people. Because I've been able to grow up in the welfare system, and go through the public housing system, and go through all these government programs, and come out still in control of my own mind and thoughts, it's unusual. And it would be naive for me to try to evaluate everyone else by that standard."

Souljah is a woman of poise and intelligence. She attended Rutgers University between 1981 and 1987, majoring in history, though she didn't earn a degree. According to her publicity material, she has lectured in South Africa, Europe and the Soviet Union.

Her views on the violence in Los Angeles are, to say the least, challenging. Consider Rodney King's own televised news conference, during which he beseeched the rioters to stop. "Can we all get along?" he asked in a cracking voice. "We've got to quit. . . . It's just not right."

To many who saw this, King's appeal was heartfelt and touching. But Souljah compared it to the scene in "Roots" where Kunta Kinte is beaten and beaten until he accepts the slave name "Toby." That news conference was Rodney King saying, "My name is Toby."

"After you beat the hell out of somebody, of course they're going to submit to you," she said. "Why would I think that Rodney King, after being beaten brutally by the police, is sober-minded? Why would I think Rodney King, as a black man who has no power in this system, would think that he [could] say what he really thinks and believes? So it meant nothing to me. He's just a symbol of what has happened to our people historically.

"Rodney King is only a symbol of a million other black men that have been beaten—brutalized by the police—who didn't have what we thought was the benefit of having it on videotape. Rodney King is only a symbol of a criminal justice system that leaves 25 percent of [young] African men in this country in prison or under court supervision."

When America saw young people rampaging on the streets of Los Angeles, and buildings ablaze, and white men being dragged from their vehicles and beaten, didn't that only reinforce the presumed attitude of the Simi Valley jury—thank God for the police, the thin blue line that protects us and our property from those violent criminals?

"Black people from the underclass and the so-called lower class do not respect the institutions of white America," Souljah replied. "Which is why you can cart out as many black people on television as you want to tell [them] that was stupid. But they don't care what you say. You don't care about their lives, haven't added anything to the quality of their lives. And then [you] expect them to respond to your opinions, which mean absolutely nothing? Why would they?"

An Eye for an Eye

But the people perpetrating that violence, did they think it was wise? Was that wise, reasoned action?

And this is when she said, "Yeah, it was wise. I mean, if black people kill black people every day, why not have a week and kill white people? You understand what I'm saying?"

But what's the wisdom in it, the sense in it?

> [Souljah said,] "If black people kill black people every day, why not have a week and kill white people?"

"It's rebellion, it's revenge. You ever heard of Hammurabi's Code? Eye for an eye, a tooth for a tooth? It's revenge. I mean, that seems so simple. I don't even understand why anybody would ask me that question. You take something from me, I take something from you. You cut me, I cut you. You shoot me, I shoot you. You kill my mother, I kill your mother."

And the individuals don't matter?

"What individuals? If you killed my mother, that mattered to me. That's why I killed yours. How could the individuals not matter? You mean the white individuals, do they matter? Not if the black ones don't," she said. "Absolutely not. Why would they? If my child dies, your child dies. If my house burns down, your house burns down. An eye for an eye, a tooth for a tooth. That's what they believe. And I see why."

The temperature of the conversation was rising. Souljah was asked if her endorsement of revenge—"Revenge is acceptable, yes"—was outweighed by any sort of transcendent respect for human life.

"Am I human?" she said sharply. "Do they kill us? Do they kill us and beat us? Police. Did they kill Latasha Harlins, did the Koreans kill her? They killed her, and they were convicted of the crime. They did not one day in jail. The Korean woman did not one day in jail."

Grocer Soon Ja Du was convicted of voluntary manslaughter in the 1991 shooting of teenager Latasha Harlins in a dispute over a bottle of orange juice. She was sentenced to probation, a fine and community service. That shooting, like the King beating, was captured on videotape by a store security camera, though much of America didn't see it until after the riots.

But did all the Korean merchants in Los Angeles kill that girl?

"No, but guess what? Then the Koreans, if they don't want to be lumped in the same pot they should have condemned and moved to prosecute that woman. And shown that they gave a damn about African life. But when they didn't, they verified that that was okay, and brought on themselves that which they received."

Would, then, any degree of "revenge" have been morally acceptable to Sister Souljah?

"This is my statement: I don't think that anything we can do to white people could ever even equal up to what they've done to us. I really don't," she said. To her, apparently, racism is original sin. White people are born guilty. And there's no Redeemer.

"Will I condemn the people for what they did in Los Angeles? No, I don't condemn them for that," she said. "In the real world, black people die on a daily basis. Always rooted in the hands of white supremacy. That's what I know."

The discussion came to an end when Souljah refused to address a hypothetical question: "Had you been there at the time, would you have struck a match?"

Note:

1. Howard Beach refers to a mostly white suburb of Queens, New York, in which one African American man was killed and another beaten in December 1986. Bensonhurst refers to another white New York City community in which a sixteen-year-old African American was shot to death on August 23, 1989. Tawana Brawley is an African-American woman who in 1987, at the age of fifteen, received national media attention for falsely accusing six white men, some of whom were police officers, of having raped her. The artist may be referring to Latasha Harlins, a fifteen-year-old African American girl who was shot and killed while exiting a South Central Los Angeles liquor store following a dispute over payment for orange juice. Soon Ja Du was found guilty of manslaughter and given probation. Some claim that because the incident followed shortly after the 1991 Rodney King beating, it contributed to the 1992 Los Angeles riots.

A Sociology Professor Reveals Riot Violence Victims and Their Rescuers

Linda Ellis

Although chaos appeared to reign in Los Angeles on April 29, 1992, some Los Angeles citizens risked their lives to rescue victims of riot violence. Ten years later, a sociology professor relates the stories of these heroes. Four African Americans who witnessed the savage beating of Reginald Denny on television left the safety of their homes to come to his aid. According to an emergency room doctor, they saved his life. When the police ignored pleas to help beating victim Takoa Hirata, another hero realized no one was coming to help. Unable to turn back, he ensured that Hirata got to a hospital. The police were able to help a journalist who had been shot several times, but only after another group of heroic citizens drove him away from the riot-torn neighborhood. The

SOURCE. Linda Ellis, "Heroic Rescuers of the 1992 Los Angeles Rebellion: An Altruistic Response to Violence," *Paths of Learning,* Issue no. 13, Summer 2002, pp. 47–48, 51. Copyright © 2002 by Linda Ellis. All rights reserved. Reproduced by permission.

surviving journalist claims that even in the midst of the violence and destruction, there was much good. Linda Ellis is a sociology professor at College of the Redwoods.

April 29, 2002 marked the tenth anniversary of the 1992 Los Angeles Rebellion. Fifty-one people lost their lives in the five-day rebellion that injured 2,383; caused over 600 fires; led to the arrest of 15,000 people; and at least $785 million in property damage breaking all previous records for American civil unrest.

In 1993 Haki R. Madhubuti stated in *Why L.A. Happened: Implications of the '92 Los Angeles Rebellion* that:

> The rebellions in L.A. and other cities in the country were not aberrations but unsophisticated and uncoordinated reactions to injustice and political/economic frustrations. Street culture took over and guided much of the response to the Simi Valley decision. When a community doesn't have culturally conscious and committed institutions—family, church, political, and economic—in a time of street crisis or calm, it is left to its own survival instincts. In this case, the streets won, we lost, confusing our expectations and shortening many of our lives.

Caught Unaware in the Rebellion

The rebellion of 1992 was triggered by a Simi Valley jury's acquittal of four white police officers who were captured on video tape inflicting 56 blows in 81 seconds to Rodney King's unresisting body after he led police officers on a high speed chase. Another beating was captured on video and beamed into American homes as they watched Los Angeles erupt. A 33-year old truck driver named Reginald Denny was on his way back to the company lot with his 18-wheeler double-loaded gravel truck when he entered the intersection of Florence and Normandie. He was unaware that a rebellion was taking place, and was forced to stop his truck because another truck had blocked one of the lanes. Two young African American men quickly opened Denny's truck door and pulled him out, beating and kicking him viciously. One of the men grabbed a brick and hit Denny in the head as another grabbed the truck's fire extinguisher and bashed his face in with such force that it pushed his eyeballs back into his fractured skull.

A Japanese American named Takoa Hirata pulled into the same intersection and waited for the light to change unaware of the danger he had driven into. As the light changed and he began moving, people started throwing bottles and bricks at his truck. He stopped his truck, so as not to injure others, and a group of young African American men ran toward him throwing and smashing bottles into his face. As the first bottle hit, he was unable to protect himself. He quickly lost consciousness and fell into his steering wheel. He was jerked back and received several more blows to the head.

A reporter named Jeff Kramer, a free-lance writer for *The Boston Globe,* found himself caught in the midst of the rebellion covering the story. Kramer soon discovered that being a reporter did not necessarily mean he was safe. He was a white man in an area where a minority rebellion was occurring. As he drove his car down Normandie Avenue, his car was pelted with rocks and bottles. When he stopped his car because of the entourage, his assailants rocked the car. They told him to get out of the car. He tried to explain that he was a reporter and even showed them his credentials. They didn't care. As he struggled to get out of the car, his seat belt would not open. One of his attackers started beating him in the face, slamming his head into the steering wheel. Kramer thought that if he played dead they would leave. The assailants hit him a few more times and then he heard a loud noise. He realized that the noise came from a gun and he had been shot in both of his legs. As the mob moved away he realized that his car was still running and he was able to move one of his injured legs enough to push the gas pedal. He hit the gas pedal and turned down a side street. Shots rang out again and he was hit in the shoulder. With both of his tires shot out, he was able to drive a few more blocks and managed to turn down another side street where he saw children playing. He stopped his car.

> " The innocent victims caught in the rebellion could have died if it were not for members of the south central Los Angeles community who risked their own lives to save them. "

Transcending the Violence

As Haki Madhubuti stated, the street violence had "won" during the rebellion but it did not "win" all of the battles. These innocent victims caught in the rebellion could have died if it were not for members of the south central Los Angeles community who risked their own lives to save them. The heroic rescuers were able to transcend the violence, anger, despair, and hopelessness found in South Central Los Angeles to save the lives of diverse strangers. During the rebellion, unlike the heroic rescue efforts of firemen and police officers during the terrorist attack on 9-11, it wasn't the police officers or firemen who were out on the streets rescuing the victims caught in the chaos. It was members of the community who reached out and saved lives.

Four African Americans left the safety of their homes to travel to the intersection of Florence and Normandie to rescue Reginald Denny. Ms. Yuille was at her mother's house in their south central Los Angeles neighborhood as she watched the beating on television. Her family had also lived through the Watts riots nearly 30 years ago. Yuille told her brother, "We've got to help him, we're Christians." She and her brother jumped into the car and headed down into the carnage. Another truck driver, Mr. Green, and his brother also talked about helping out and drove down to try to help. Green's brother dropped him

FATALITIES FROM THE 1992 LOS ANGELES RIOTS	
Total dead	53
By cause of death	
Gunshot wounds	35
Shot by law enforcement	8
Shot by National Guardsmen	2
Arson fires	6
Hit with sticks or boards	2
Stab wounds	2
Car accidents	6
Hit and runs	2
By racial category	
African Americans	25
Latino/a	16
White	8
Southeast Asian	2
North African	1
South Asian	1
Middle Eastern	1
By sex	
Men	48
Women	5
Unsolved riot-related homicides	22

off at the gas station and headed home. As Green ran through the crowd trying to get to Denny, his gold chain was ripped off his neck along with his watch, which was snatched from his wrist.

Driving into the Madness

Mr. Murphy and Ms. Barnett were at home watching the beating on television. They decided to drive down to see if they could help Denny. The only problem they faced was what to do with Barnett's 8-year-old daughter. They decided to put her on the floorboard of the back seat as they drove down into the madness.

When Yuille arrived on the scene, Denny had somehow pulled himself back into his truck and was trying to drive away. She tried to get Denny to pull the truck over to the curb. He just kept trying to drive. Murphy and Barnett sped into the intersection and parked the car as Mr. Murphy rushed over to Denny's truck. Yuille told Murphy that Denny was still alive. Murphy decided to drive the truck to the hospital because Denny needed immediate medical attention. Murphy rushed over to Barnett and told her the plan and asked her to drive ahead and run interference for them. As Murphy headed back to the truck he noticed a man running through the crowd toward Denny's truck. He and Yuille feared this man was going to finish Denny off. It was Green, who told them that he was a truck driver and that he would drive the truck. Murphy agreed, as it had been at least fifteen years since he had driven a double-loaded truck. It took time for the rig to speed up. Two police cars drove by in the opposite direction and the rescuers waved, honked the horn, and tried to catch their attention. Murphy even stood on top of the rig waving his arms and yelling, but the police did not stop. As the truck sped up Denny asked them, "Why? Why did they do this?"

When Yuille, Green, Murphy, and Barnett arrived at the hospital the emergency room was overflowing.

Denny was spitting up blood and went into convulsions before they could get him out [of] the truck. They rushed into the emergency room and managed to get help. Later, the rescuers were told by Denny's doctor that, had they arrived a minute later, he would have died.

Chaos Reigns

On his way home from the gym Gregory Alan-Williams heard on the radio that Whites, Asians, and Latinos were being targeted and beaten during the rebellion, so he turned his car around and drove to the scene to see if he could help someone, anyone. He came upon Mr. Hirata, who was being beaten by young African American men, who had started throwing and smashing bottles into Mr. Hirata's face. When he saw this utter brutality being inflicted upon Mr. Hirata, Alan-Williams jumped out of his car and walked up to the perpetrators and said, "Come on ya'll . . . ya'll know this ain't right." The assailants paused for a moment and at the same time there was some kind of disturbance going on that diverted the attackers enough for Alan-Williams to pull Hirata from his truck. When Hirata gained consciousness, Alan-Williams told him that he had to try to walk or he was going to die. As the two struggled down the street a police cruiser passed by and Alan-Williams hailed them for help. He told them that Mr. Hirata was seriously injured. The black police officer behind the wheel and the white female partner were silent. They stared at Hirata and Alan-Williams for twenty or thirty seconds and then drove away. It became clear to Alan-Williams that chaos reigned. Later in *A Gathering of Heroes,* he stated, "At that point it was very clear to me there would be no Calvary, and John Wayne wasn't coming and neither was Wesley Snipes."

> It was very clear . . . there would be no Cavalry, and John Wayne wasn't coming and neither was Wesley Snipes.

Lei Yuille, Terri Barnett, Titus Murphy, and Gregory Alan Williams (right to left) are welcomed as heroes by the Los Angeles City Council on May 5, 1992, for their bravery in rescuing truck driver Reginald Denny during the first night of the riots. (© **AP Photo/Bob Galbraith**.)

Unable to Turn Back

He couldn't turn back. Mr. Hirata was bleeding from his left ear and Alan-Williams knew that he had to get him to the hospital as soon as possible. A man stopped in a van and asked Mr. Alan-Williams if he needed him to take Hirata to the hospital. Alan-Williams wasn't sure if this man was trustworthy. Alan-Williams asked him, "You sure, man? You're gonna take him to the hospital, right?" He responded, "For real, Black. For real." Alan-Williams agreed, and the young man drove Hirata to Daniel Freeman Hospital. Mr. Hirata survived.

When Jeff Kramer stopped his car, he asked the children he heard playing if they would get their parents because he had been shot. The children froze, but fortunately someone else had heard his plea. Mr. Guidroz rushed out of his mother's house to the car where Kramer lay injured, when his sister told him that a man had been shot. Guidroz's mother immediately called 911. To protect Kramer, they lowered the back seat of his car to get him out of sight. Whenever a car came by they covered his head with blankets. Unfortunately, after waiting 30 to 40 minutes, they realized the paramedics were not coming. A neighbor offered to drive Kramer to the hospital. Guidroz, his mother, and the neighbor helped him out of his car and put him in the back seat of the car. As they were going down Martin Luther King, Jr. Boulevard, they saw a police car, and pulled alongside the car, and told the officers' they had a reporter in the car that had been shot. The police were able to flag down an ambulance and Mr. Kramer was taken to the hospital. . . .

> As much as getting shot may have rocked my faith in humanity, my rescuers restored it—and then some.

As we remember the tenth anniversary of the 1992 Los Angeles rebellion and the violence and destruction that ensued, may we also remember the heroic acts of the rescuers who lived their principles and uplifted humanity. Kramer expressed this sentiment upon being reunited with Guidroz, his rescuer, when he wrote in *People Weekly,* "There is a lot of good in South Central too. As much as getting shot may have rocked my faith in humanity, my rescuers restored it—and then some."

CHAPTER 2

Controversies Surrounding the 1992 Los Angeles Riots

The 1992 Los Angeles Riots Were a Racial Rebellion

Brenda Wall

In the following viewpoint, a clinical psychologist maintains that the violence that erupted in 1992 Los Angeles was a race riot. Indeed, she argues, the rage was a direct response to the systemic harassment of African Americans by the police and the United States' failure to address entrenched racism—a system of white oppression in which whites continue to profit at the expense of African Americans. In the face of widely viewed video evidence, she maintains that the acquittal of four white Los Angeles police officers for the brutal beating of Rodney King demonstrates that the legal system fosters racism by marginalizing and silencing its victims. In fact, she concludes, white America's effort to occupy the riot-torn Los Angeles community and assign all of the blame to the rioters reflects the country's failure to heal its racial

Photo on previous page: Many stores in Los Angeles, such as the ABC Market in South Central, were ransacked and looted by rioters on April 29, 1992. (© **AP Photo/Paul Sakuma.**)

SOURCE. Brenda Wall, "Chapter Two: Inexact Justice," *Rodney King Rebellion: A Psychopolitical Analysis of Racial Despair and Hope.* Chicago: African American Images, 1992, pp. 10–13, 17–21, 25–26.

wounds. Brenda Wall is the author of *The Rodney King Rebellion: A Psychopolitical Analysis of Racial Despair and Hope.*

America was shocked when confronted with the Rodney King beating. It was cruel. It was senseless. It was unnecessary. There seemed to be some sick satisfaction by the policemen in their brutal show of power and control. It was too graphic a picture of White racism. Surely, this was not a part of civilized America. Unfortunately, many African American men were able to relate to the image of Rodney King being savagely beaten and totally unable to stop it. They knew about it because they had lived it. Rodney King represented what happened to many African American men when they encountered police. Not all the beatings were as violent, but they sometimes were. Not all the incidents were reported, but they sometimes were. Whether the incidents were verbal harassment or physical abuse, questionable or extreme, they tended to be handled with the same routine. It usually did not matter what the victims reported in such an institutionally entrenched atmosphere of racism. The faces became invisible and the voices became silenced. The kinship with apartheid South Africa was evident in style, statistics and denial.

The Impact of the Rodney King Beating

The difference with Rodney King was that everybody saw it. He had a broken, beaten face. His image lingered. He was visibly real and he evoked sympathy. Even so, there arose a consistent effort to neutralize the criticism of the police department that produced the perpetrators and the victim. From the president of the country to the chief of police, there was a steady, reinforced effort to maintain the system of law enforcement as it presently functioned. There was never a focus on remedy, but instead on maintaining power and control, on law and order. There was no kinder and gentler concern towards Rodney King or towards the community victimized by riots. Instead there was a foreboding guarantee that reactive community violence would be controlled. The violence of the police department never generated as much interest. Therein lay the problem and the double standard.

Americans become confused when there is a breakdown in its rigid management of embarrassing racism. Law and order provide the ideal cover-up for patriotic actions that are criminal and immoral. As long as African American men can be criminalized, they can be presented as deserving their plight. It is then possible to use the very system that provides service and protection to some parts of the community, as a tool of repression and degradation in the inner cities of America.

The embarrassment forces a duality in which Republicans can blame Democrats, more jails can be argued against more human resources, and self-reliance can be pitted against compensation for damages. All are based on strategies that never address the needs of the marginalized underclass. Whether more jails are built or more welfare services are created, establishment America seems to have no intention of removing the community of victims or even the individual victims of abuse.

> The Rodney King verdict illustrated the norm, not the exception, as it is seen by many African Americans.

The Rodney King verdict illustrated the norm, not the exception, as it is seen by many African Americans. The brief glimpse of this dynamic by mainstream Americans created a shocking disbelief and a possible realization that something is gravely wrong.

A New Kind of Slavery

Whether from jails, from welfare programs, or from drug traffic, establishment America continues to insist

Maxine Waters: Controversial Congressional Representative of South Central Los Angeles

Considered by many the most powerful black woman in American politics, Maxine Waters has been a member of the U.S. House of Representatives since 1991. After a distinguished career as a legislator in California—where she was known as a staunch defender of the rights of African Americans, women, and the poor—Waters won election to the Congressional seat being vacated by octogenarian fellow-Democrat Augustus F. Hawkins. Throughout her career in politics, Waters has been famous for her outspoken and confrontational manner, and her persistence in pursuing the interests of her constituency. As she told *Essence* magazine in November 1990, "If you believe in something, you must be prepared to fight. To argue. To persuade. To introduce legislation again and again and again. . . . Too many Black politicians want to be in the mainstream. . . . My power comes from the fact that I am ready to talk about Black people.". . .

Throughout her career in Congress, Waters has been a magnet for controversy. Near the end of her first term, [the 1992 Los Angeles riots] broke out in Waters' district. . . . While Waters was one of the first federal officers to arrive in the riot zone and offer aid, she came under fire for remarks that seemed to justify the looting of Korean-owned businesses. Congresswoman Waters was unapologetic: "I said in a 101 different ways that violence is not right, that I do not condone violence, that people cannot endanger their own or others' lives. What I didn't do is to use the airwaves to call people hoodlums and thugs for burning down their own communities. It only makes them madder when you call them hoodlums and thugs, as the President did.". . .

Waters considers herself an inspiration to average women, maintaining that if she can succeed, so can they. "People who come from backgrounds like mine are not supposed to serve in the U.S. Congress," she asserted in *Essence*. "When a little girl who came out of poverty in St. Louis has an opportunity to serve in Congress, it is like thumbing your nose at the status quo." In Washington Waters continues to fight for black interests with the same forcefulness and skill she has demonstrated for more than thirty years.

SOURCE. *"Maxine Waters,"* Contemporary Black Biography, *vol. 67. Gale, 2008. Copyright © 1998 by Cengage Learning.*

on reaping an economic profit from its deceptive management of the underclass. Benevolent management, indifferent management, or stark abuse—the parallels cause many to conclude that this system which results in profits for the establishment, at the expense of those locked out of the system is merely a new kind of slavery.

Missing from this skewed system is the input from those who have been made invisible and silent. They bring into focus obvious injustices and suggest one practical solution in the rejection of roles assigned to the marginalized underclass. The implication of eliminating oppression of marginalized America requires a shift in the balance of power. It represents an economic threat for those in control of the establishment and a moral dilemma for those who defensively cry that they have never done anything to contribute to this tragedy. If there were no profits from the drug economy or from the maintenance economy—that in itself would cause a shift in the distribution of wealth. Empowering the marginalized would contribute to a new balance of power. Thus, in order to maintain the status quo, it becomes imperative that the marginalized voices be kept silenced, the faces be kept invisible and the arguments for fairness be kept non-credible. . . .

The Pathology of Racism

Americans have difficulty comprehending the looting, the destruction of African America's own community (instead of Beverly Hills, for example), or the rage against Whites. Actually, these questions have been answered previously, after every major race riot that has occurred this century. The riot commissions which followed eleven different incidents of "urban disorder" over the last several decades have reached the same broad conclusions. Comprised of prominent White male leaders for the most part, these commissions have thoroughly documented the conditions which lead to violence. The last time America listened in earnest for these answers was in response to the Watts riots of 1965.

Yet, you would think from the simplistic questions that America has never before known race riots, never before heard of the Kerner Commission Report, or never before studied the characteristics of mob hysteria. Americans still refuse to accept the debilitating influence of racism and economic immobilization. Riots are not a solution to the problem, nor are they a rational and strategic use of power. Most rioters are not criminally motivated to break law and order. It is important to understand that the riots which occurred after the King verdict are symptoms of a chronic social pathology. Riots are an embodiment of that pathology—a pathology which lies in establishment America.

Criminalization and Containment

Rodney King has become as much a part of American history as Dred Scott[1] or even Martin Luther King, Jr., because all reflect the refusal of establishment America to address her unresolved racial pathology. Instead, political control and economic exploitation, which started here in 1619, are the heralded method of managing racism. Racism is immoral, impractical, dysfunctional, and costly, but it is a part of the repressive elements that exist in American history. White America resists learning new and positive approaches of handling racism. Instead, denial and control persist. Evidence of increased police repression in Los Angeles was apparent in the emergency legislation enacted to extend the time for arraignment after the insurrection and also in the arbitrary detention of those accused of participating in the Los Angeles riots. This is but one mechanism utilized to occupy a community which has

> Rodney King has become as much a part of American history as Dred Scott or even Martin Luther King, Jr.

already been devastated—by maximizing control instead of alleviating the underlying social tragedies. The degree of community instability makes it hard to focus on the dangerous process of criminalization and containment. Thus, a potential for racial genocide is already in place.

The pathology of racism damages the targeted victim. Many of those who rioted felt powerless and expressed their overwhelming helplessness and frustration in an uncontrollable rage and an effort to demonstrate personal and collective power. Those who had been damaged by policies of contempt and neglect, cried out for justice. For a public which has become sensitive enough not to debate suicide but respond by supplying professional help, there is an amazing ignorance and denial when such suicidal dynamics are manifest on a group dimension. Instead of "professional help," the thousands of people who participated in the riots are criminalized in an effort to further control their actions.

> The thousands of people who participated in the riots are criminalized in an effort to further control their actions.

As frightening and disturbing as riots are, it is even more frightening and disturbing to live with the reality that the social pathology does not originate with the victim. Those who looted, burned and cried out are not all fundamentally pathological. The sickness originates elsewhere. The need to racially subordinate a group of people by unlimited force, and then to be totally unable and unwilling to stop and accept responsibility for the sick and abusive process is the source of the problem.

Rejecting Oppression

The war on African American men has become clear to more people, partly because of increased cultural exposure and growing political awareness. The pervasive threat from establishment America is more easily

A photo of Rodney King taken March 6, 1991, shows some of the injuries he sustained when several Los Angeles police officers beat him three days earlier. (© **AP Photo/ Pool, File.**)

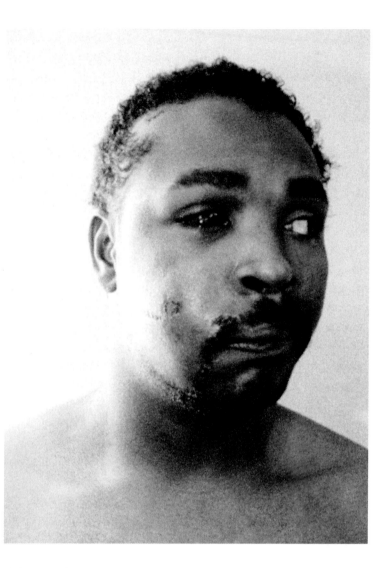

delineated, resulting in renewed suspicion and a readiness to do something. Those who understand the King response as rebellion are interpreting the spontaneous African American movement to reject this oppression. The strategy and the tactics are still in the formative stages. Riot and rebellion were both operative in the King aftermath. A riot can be interpreted as including the self-destructive components of individuals and community who may have hurt themselves; but rebellion was clearly reflected as an aspect of power directed towards fuller expression. It was a refusal to accept the rules which oppress. This generation of African Americans has the same bitterness, the same rhetoric and maybe even the same insight into racial oppression which has been historically present. The rage and bitterness are familiar, but there is a new capacity for retaliation caused by the unprecedented drug infiltration. The Vietnam veterans of the 1960s boasted of their combat training, but the gangs of the 1990s can boast a firepower and organization which poses a great threat in the event of recurring riot or insurrection.

It is significant that the Crips and the Bloods, powerful gang rivals, were able to unite and work together in providing protection during the riots—a protection that the police were unable or unwilling to provide. Their commitment to unity is not remarkable because there now exists a new "super" African American Gang. New, because it represents an unprecedented movement away from intra-community division and conflict. This gang unity is both inhibiting to impulsive police attacks and is potentially valuable for a new perspective on police occupation and community oppression.

The police have made their next move by labeling one out of two African American men as possibly gang-involved and are planning to deal with them accordingly. The next step for the oppressed can be seen in the development of direction, strategy and a renewed vision. Ongoing riots are ultimately self-defeating; rebellion, however, is not. Rebellion has paved the way for American independence, South African negotiation and historical and contemporary empowerment throughout the world. . . .

Awakening from Denial

The civil rights songs of overcoming symbolize failure and are rejected by many of today's youth. It has been replaced by political rap with its hostile lyrics. This contemporary music form represents today's generation's effort to direct and motivate itself. Since 1619, African resistance has alternated with African American denial. Some youth today have awakened from denial to the reality that racism and oppression continue to dominate. Racial oppression has recently gone unchallenged by the masses. Many were seduced into denial by the material and social opportunities made possible by the civil rights era. The mass action subsided. Malcolm X had only one voice, not ten, and when he was silenced, protest of racial oppression was dramatically splintered. Although some have suggested that there are generational conflicts which contributed to the riots, there has been no actual generation gap in racial empowerment. No generation has significantly defeated racism or betrayed the next one. No generation has escaped the personal and community destruction of racism. Instead there is more of a generational continuity where all are linked by the incomplete defeat of racial oppression. The civil rights generation did not fail us; the segregation generation did not fail us nor did the post-Reconstruction generation. All eras have allowed us to more clearly articulate the problem. We did not fail ourselves. America has failed us. African Americans have not completed their work towards a very necessary victory. It is necessary for the survival of African Americans and probably for the very survival of America. Not completing the victory is not the same as failure.

Some would also suggest that the Rodney King verdict triggered a class riot, not a race riot. Many losses were sustained by Koreans, Latinos, and Anglos; all participated in the looting as well. However, it is important to recognize that the King verdict ignited a

> The King verdict ignited a unique dynamic in the African American community which related to police harassment in particular and overwhelming racial oppressions in general. This was a race riot.

unique dynamic in the African American community which related to police harassment in particular and overwhelming racial oppression in general. This was a race riot. However, establishment's failure to resolve her racial wounds is reflected in other self-defeating policy outcomes which have resulted in other areas of weakness. America does have an emerging class issue, some of which could be seen in the Los Angeles riots. America has many domestic problems which were reflected in the riot: but reducing it to a class riot would serve to cloud the specific problem.

Note:

1. Dred Scott was an African American slave who unsuccessfully sued for his freedom in the 1857 US Supreme Court case *Dred Scott v. Sanford*.

The 1992 Los Angeles Riots Were a Political Revolution

Grover Furr

In the following viewpoint, a professor argues that the violence that erupted in 1992 Los Angeles was a revolt against an exploitive government, not a race riot. After years of being kept in their place by a repressive police force, the residents of South Central Los Angeles finally erupted in fury following the acquittal of four police officers for the use of excessive force in the beating of Rodney King. Nevertheless, with media help, the government continues to exploit and divide working Americans by painting the rebellion as a race riot, he contends. Although the violence and devastation are lamentable, the author believes violent disruptions are sometimes necessary to break the yoke of oppression. Grover Furr is an English professor who specializes in Marxist literature, the Communist movement, and social and political protest at Montclair State University in New Jersey.

SOURCE. Grover Furr, "Welcome to the Rebellions!," *Canadian Dimension*, vol. 26, no. 5, July–August 1992, p. 8. Copyright © 1992 by Grover C. Furr. All rights reserved. Reproduced by permission.

Throughout the world millions of workers recognize the LA rebellions as something that is good for them, too. Like the German workers we, too—American students and working people—should welcome and support the rebellions in Los Angeles and other major US cities.

They were touched off by the acquittal of the four racist LA cops whose brutal beating of Rodney King could not be denied because millions have seen it. In a verdict worthy of South Africa or Nazi Germany, the jury found the cops were only "doing their job." Ironically, the jury was right: the cops' job is to keep the most oppressed and exploited section of the black working class in their place by a constant reign of terror. The King verdict was just the last and most blatant outrage that released the floodgates of anger.

> "It is always inspiring when oppressed people rise up in fury."

Unmasking the Horror of Exploitation

It is always inspiring when oppressed people rise up in fury. Rebellions such as this lift the cloak of propaganda and respectability that masks the naked horror of exploitation and murder, and let us see the rage and despair this oppression causes. It would have been terrible if, faced with the King verdict, there had been no rebellions. Like the intifada of the Palestinian workers against Israeli fascism, the 15-year uprisings in the South African ghettos against apartheid, and the Soviet workers' recent strikes and demonstrations against the brutal attack on their standard of living by the Yeltsin regime, the rebels of Los Angeles, Atlanta, Sacramento, and other black working-class ghettos deserve our unqualified support.

If the Caterpillar workers, who recently had a sell-out contract rammed down their throats by the United Auto Workers, had instead used the militancy and willingness to break the law, they—and we—would be much better off. If college students are ever to roll back skyrocketing tuitions; if American workers are ever to begin to beat back the cuts in jobs, wages, and health benefits that have slashed our standard of living and are destroying our children's lives, we will have to show some of the militancy and defiance of the law that the black ghetto residents have shown.

Agents of Government Propaganda

The media have abandoned any pretence at "objectivity" and have done their best to portray the rebellions as anti-white rampages or as "senseless violence," and to help "quiet things down." These are the same media that sympathetically portray nationalist revolts in Eastern Europe and fascist Afghani guerrillas, but never fail to depict strikes in the US in an anti-worker light.

As usual in crises, the media have once again shown that they follow the government party line, almost as though they were government propaganda agents. In fact, just a year ago, during the Gulf War, the media were also feeding up US government propaganda. In times of crisis, the media show themselves for what they really are—not independent seekers of the truth, but obedient servants to oppressive power. Another example: since April 24 [1992] there has been a sit-in at Brown University, led by a multi-racial student group, to demand more admission of black and low-income students. The media have ignored it totally.

> What really terrifies the US ruling class is that white workers will take their cue from the ghetto rebels.

The main aspect of the rebellions—not "riots"—has been fury at the cops, the visible repressive force in the cities, and at the politicians. It is a significant and hopeful sign that the revolt occurred in the US city that has had a black mayor for the longest time. For it was after the

ghetto rebellions of the 1960s that the Democratic Party moved to put black politicians in charge of the major US cities to "keep them cool." Black workers are now seeing through that nationalist tactic.

What really terrifies the US ruling class is that white workers will take their cue from the ghetto rebels. If white workers and students were to cast aside racism and unite with black and Latin workers, the days of the Bush Administration, and in fact the whole system of exploitation, would be numbered.

A man breaks a door of the criminal courts building in downtown Los Angeles on April 29, 1992, in reaction to the verdict in the Rodney King trial. (© Hal Garb/AFP/ Getty Images.)

This Is Not a Racial Rebellion

Racism is the main ideology, the "false consciousness" that keeps US workers oppressed and exploited. It is the "divide and conquer" strategy, the main tactic of ruling classes since the Roman Empire. So the media push the elite's line, just as they did during the Gulf War a year ago, and portray the rebellion as anti-white, instead of anti-cop and anti-government.

Naturally, there have been some incidents of racism against whites, Koreans, and others. How could there not be? Since the 1670s racism has been deliberately created—there was virtually none before that time—in order to divide white and black workers so that both might be exploited freely by the elite.

What of the liberal experts? We should beware of those who claim to "understand the despair" of the "rioters" but focus on the relatively few, though deplorable, incidents of racism. Most of them would prefer no rebellions at all! What the rest of us need is better, more effective, more militant rebellions—free of racism, directed against the seats of state power, the cops and the government. We are glad to see such rebellions in oppressive foreign lands; we should be even more ready to welcome them, and indeed to help them, in our own country.

Likewise, looting and arson show, not a "criminal" mentality, but a short-sighted one, attacking the exploiters near at hand rather than the system itself. But really democratic, popular uprisings, such as the American, French, Russian and Chinese revolutions, never occur without such disruptions. Those who claim to want a popular uprising pure of any destruction really do not want them at all. As Friedrich Engels said, they "want an ocean without the rush of its mighty waters."

The ghetto rebellions of the '60s forced many gains in US society. Without them, we at MSC [Montclair State College] would have no E.O.F. [Educational Opportunity Fund] program, thanks to which thousands of black, Latin, and also white working class students have gone to college who never would have. But because they did not result in a popular, anti-racist, working class movement independent of both political parties and dedicated to fundamental political change, the rebellions of the

1960s, like the anti-war movement, dissipated, and their gains have been eroded.

From Moscow to Peru to Los Angeles, working people are fighting back against their oppression. We should support this, because it is our fight. We can start by fighting racism—the ideology that, above all others, divides white and black workers and students from each other, and guarantees that our struggles will fail.

> From Moscow to Peru to Los Angeles, working people are fighting back against their oppression.

The 1992 Los Angeles Riots Are a Symbol of Urban Decay

Jean Dimeo

In the following viewpoint, a building industry journalist argues that urban problems that sparked the 1992 Los Angeles riots mirror problems faced by many cities nationwide. Large cities have more high-school dropouts, drugs, and poverty, while few have access to low-income homes, the author explains. Some politicians argue that reduction in federal aid to inner cities led to the conditions in South Los Angeles in 1992. However, others claim that simply throwing money at cities will not resolve urban problems. Although lawmakers differ on how to spend federal resources on urban problems, most support laws that will create jobs, promote business, improve public safety and schools, and encourage minority loans. Jean Dimeo is editor in chief of *Builder* magazine.

SOURCE. Jean Dimeo, "Fiddling While the Country Burns," *American City & County,* July 1992, p. 12. Copyright © 1992 by American City & County. All rights reserved. Reproduced by permission.

It took a riot in Los Angeles for President Bush and lawmakers to wake up to the plight of American cities.

"For the past decade, attempts have been made to sweep our urban areas under the carpet," said Sen. Chris Dodd (D-Conn.) during a recent heating on urban woes. "Regrettably, we are now paying the price of that neglect."

Decaying Cities

Local government leaders say the Los Angeles crisis was not a reaction to the Rodney King verdict; instead, it was a desperate cry for reinvestment in decaying cities.

"While it was L.A. that was up in flames, we know deep in our hearts it could have been any city in America," says Boston Mayor Raymond Flynn, immediate past president of the U.S. Conference of Mayors. Republicans blamed the Los Angeles ordeal on failings of the '60s' Great Society programs, while Democrats point fingers at Republican presidents of the last 12 years. Still, most agree the current system—no matter whose fault—needs repair.

> The Los Angeles crisis was not a reaction to the Rodney King verdict . . . it was a desperate cry for reinvestment in decaying cities.

While the riot has given urgency to local governments' long-standing pleas for help, it does not guarantee that Washington will give back the federal aid it took away during the past decade. Nor is there any evidence that federal spending on cities will ever approach past levels. Congressional Democrats and Republicans struck a fragile accord—a least one of cordial words—about working together to help America's inner cities. They are, however, far apart on many issues, including how much financial aid should be funneled to localities.

Democrats are pushing for billions of dollars. "It's clear our cities can't survive without an infusion of money," says Sen. John Kerry (D-Mass.).

However, many Republicans disagree. "An infusion of money into our cities is not going to solve our problems," says Sen. Alfonse D'Amato (R-N.Y.) "I'm not suggesting they don't need more resources, but what we should look at is what has caused the loss of jobs. Just throwing money to the mayors isn't going to solve the exodus of jobs."

The Problems in Los Angeles Are Mirrored Nationwide

In testimony before Congress, developer James Rouse, chairman of The Enterprise Foundation, a non-profit organization that builds low-income housing, said the problems in Los Angeles that sparked the riots are mirrored nationwide:

- More poverty—25 million Americans in the mid-'70s were poor versus 34 million today;

- Fewer low-income homes—housing for $250 a month or less has declined 41 percent since the late '70s;

- More homeless—100,000 children live on the streets or shelters;

- More high school dropouts—as high as 30 percent to 40 percent in urban city schools;

- More drugs—25 percent of the babies born in inner-city hospital are drug-addicted at birth.

"This is America. Can you believe it?" says Rouse, whose festival marketplace developments have revitalized a number of declining urban centers.

But while lawmakers and the president quickly pledged millions of dollars to rebuild Los Angeles, Congress was authorizing Bush's orders to spend billions on B2 stealth bombers and aid to the former Soviet Union—sore points with many local leaders.

"The federal government can't solve all our problems, but there should be a new commitment," says Baltimore

PHYSICAL DAMAGE TO BUILDINGS DURING THE 1992 LOS ANGELES RIOTS

Value of Damage	$446 billion
Number of Buildings Damaged	**1,120**
Commercial	1,050
Residential	98
Level of Damage	
Number of buildings destroyed	**377**
Number of buildings seriously damaged *	**222**
Types of Buildings Damaged **	
Commercial	**1,008**
Retail	764
Restaurant	70
Gas station	58
Office	57
Manufacturing	17
Warehouse	11
Public garage	10
Private garage	7
Hotel	5
Church	5
Theater	2
Public office	2
Residential	**85**
Single family dwelling	29
Duplex	7
Apartment	29
Other	20

* Seriously damaged is defined as 50 percent or more of the building is damaged.
** Total by building type is less than the total number of buildings damaged because not all buildings are classified by type.

Data compiled from: Community Redevelopment Agency of the City of Los Angeles, Profile of 1992 Civil Disturbance Damage and Areas of Need, City of Los Angeles, Department of City Planning, September 1992.

Taken from: Denise DiPasquale and Edward Glaeser, "The Los Angeles Riot and the Economics of Urban Unrest," *Journal of Urban Economics*, vol. 43, no. 1, January 1998.

Hundreds of homeless people in Los Angeles wait in line for food in 1992. Some argue that the economic recession of the early 1990s, decreased federal aid for inner-city neighborhoods, increased unemployment, and poverty fueled the 1992 riots. (© **AP Photo/Bob Galbraith.**)

Mayor Kurt Schmoke, a Democrat. "The president wants to spend only $2.3 billion on cities; that's a national shame."

A Shift to Urban Programs

Local officials are pushing many federal-aid proposals, including:

- Enacting bills that funnel money and jobs into programs aimed at improving public safety, social services, education, housing and transportation. One such package includes funding more than 7,000 "ready-to-go" infrastructure projects that could put 250,000 Americans to work;

- Creating enterprise zones that give tax breaks and other incentives to firms locating in depressed areas;

- Amending the Community Reinvestment Act so that more loans go to minorities, low-income families and small businesses;

- Reforming the Job Training Partnership Act so that the very poor and the poorly educated get real training and real jobs;

- Fully funding Head Start; and, finally,

- Prohibiting unfunded state and federal mandates. The White House, which is lukewarm to most of these ideas except enterprise zones, wants $1 billion for the HOPE home ownership program that would help tenants buy public housing units; welfare and education reforms; and a $500 million "weed and seed" proposal that targets selected neighborhoods for anti-crime efforts and social service programs.

Funding presents the biggest problem for all these proposals. Congressional Democrats and mayors want to break down the budget walls so defense funds can be shifted to urban programs, but Republicans oppose the idea.

"I'm tired of listening to all these mayors say all we need to do is cut the military budget and that will solve everything," says Sen. Jake Garn (R-Utah). "At the end of five years, we'll have reduced the military to 14 percent of the budget; this is not a money pot we can keep cutting."

Despite some fundamental differences, most Republicans and Democrats agree that efforts to aid local governments must support job creation.

"Job creation is the most essential issue about solving this problem," says Sen. Donald Riegle (D-Mich.), chairman of the Senate Banking, House and & Urban Affairs Committee. "We cannot begin to make serious inroads until we begin to create jobs."

A Riot of Color: The Demographic Setting

Peter A. Morrison and Ira S. Lowry

In the following viewpoint, a demographer and a housing and development consultant dispute the general view that the 1992 Los Angeles riots were a reaction to the brutal beating of a black man by white police officers. Although the acquittal was an emotionally significant event, demographic changes in South Central Los Angeles made the community ripe for conflagration, the authors maintain. Indeed, Korean merchants were the primary targets and over half of those arrested were Hispanic. The growing number of Latinos and Asian businesses in South Central created significant ethnic tension. The authors contend that these changes, combined with a large number of unemployed young males with little education, contributed to the explosion of violence and crime. Peter A. Morrison is a demographer with the RAND

Corporation. Ira S. Lowry is a housing and development consultant in California.

When the police officers who beat Rodney King were exonerated by a predominantly white suburban jury on April 29, 1992, street corner disturbances immediately erupted in two black neighborhoods of South Central Los Angeles. Within a few hours, these disturbances escalated into a three-day riot that damaged people and property over an area of almost 60 square miles. Since then, these three days of mob violence, arson, and looting in Los Angeles have usually been represented in the press and other public forums as a political protest by blacks against manifest injustice to a fellow black, brutally mistreated by white police officers. However, a careful look at the sequence of events and the actual participants in terms of race and ethnicity suggests that this view greatly oversimplifies and misrepresents the civil tensions that erupted on April 29, 1992. Although whites who happened to be in the wrong place at the wrong time were harassed and beaten, the truly systematic targets of violence were retail establishments, ranging from neighborhood convenience stores to discount houses and supermarkets; Korean shopkeepers were especially at risk. And over half of those arrested by the Los Angeles police during six days of civil disturbance were Hispanic, not black. . . .

We adopt a demographic perspective on this "riot of color" that engulfed selected parts of metropolitan Los Angeles while leaving most of the area unscathed. Although demographic factors cannot "explain" riots, they are one salient, quantifiable facet of the tensions and

> Although whites who happened to be in the wrong place at the wrong time were harassed and beaten, the truly systematic targets of violence were retail establishments.

processes that fuel them. An understanding of the demographic setting can sharpen social science interpretations of civil unrest in cities and how it propagates.

Our analysis suggests that the local demographic setting in this instance was ripe for unrest. Ethnic tensions existed, and a large percentage of youthful men in the area were at liberty to participate. . . .

In our view, the salient *preconditions* for South Central's riot were (1) territorially based ethnic tensions and (2) an abundance of young men with time on their hands. The *occasion* for the riot was an event of deep emotional significance to many inhabitants of South Central: the acquittal of white police who beat a black arrestee. The announcement of the verdict triggered several street-corner disturbances that under other circumstances might have been self-limiting or easily contained by competently organized police action. But on April 29, 1992, the disturbances flared into three days of arson, looting, and random violence.

Although some observers insist on describing the riot as a political statement—a "rebellion" against the white power structure—we find such a description misleading. Half of those participating in the riot were Latinos, not ethnically linked to Rodney King. The rioters' primary targets were not the property of or institutions controlled by the white power structure, but retail shops owned by Koreans. A number of establishments owned by blacks and Latinos were also trashed and looted. Probation reports on those convicted of riot-related felonies clearly indicate that looting was the primary motivation for most rioters who were caught; few were consciously "political."

> "Half of those participating in the riot were Latinos, not ethnically linked to Rodney King.

Ethnically charged events, especially interethnic violence, defamatory speech, and commercial fraud, are common and perhaps inevitable features of a multiethnic society. But they seldom result in anything more than graffiti, a shouting match, or one-on-one violence. What made South Central ready for conflagration, we think, was a long accumulation of grievances against ethnically different neighbors who were accessible for reprisal, combined with the availability of a large pool of idle young men who had little stake in civil order.

Territorially Based Ethnic Tension

Territorially based ethnic tension is endemic in California and a number of other multiethnic states. In California, one of every four cities has no racial or ethnic majority; its population is composed of three large ethnic groups ("Anglo," Latino, black) and perhaps a dozen small ones (Filipinos, Koreans, Vietnamese, Hmong, Armenians, Iranians, etc.), each clustered residentially but in adjoining neighborhoods. The tides of immigration and assimilation continuously wash against the conventional boundaries of these neighborhoods, so that one's ethnic territory and ethnic identity are never entirely secure.

The salient aspects of ethnic difference include race, national origin, language, social customs, recency of arrival, and civil status (citizens, legally resident non-citizens, illegal residents). Though nearly all such groups are quick to adopt some of the values and lifestyles of the prevailing popular culture (as revealed by television) and to learn the prevailing language, most cling fiercely to their ethnic identities—that is, to their sense of a shared history and shared future that makes them responsible for each other's welfare. Ethnic identity has its roots in some historical community of people who inhabited a specific territory, developed a common language and culture, and practiced endogamy. The surprising feature of ethnic identity is its persistence for generations among those who left their homelands to mingle with

Life in South Central Los Angeles

News accounts often portray South Central L.A. as an exotic world filled with Uzi-toting gang members, promiscuous teenage girls looking for crack and innocent children who dive for cover on bullet-riddled playgrounds. To be sure, such characters and events do exist. But day-to-day life at Florence and Normandie [the site of the first reports of violence on April 29, 1992] was far more ordinary. Young males hoping to meet girls headed to Kakawana's car wash or lingered at Art's Chili Dogs next door. A half-dozen winos hung out in the parking lot at the corner at Tom's Liquor, where they were sometimes joined by a few crack addicts who occasionally hustled tips pumping gas at the Unocal 76 station across the street. And almost anyone who was hungry was welcome on 71st Street, where several moms always seemed to cook enough to feed the entire block.

To outsiders, however, the neighborhood was far more forbidding. In particular, a significant segment of residents—especially young black men—detested cops. That antagonism had grown during the 1980s, as overwork and serious understaffing forced officers to have less contact with law-abiding residents and more encounters with an ever more violent criminal underclass, leaving many officers jaded. Then, in 1988, Chief Daryl Gates launched a controversial series of gang-member roundups. In one night, 1,000 extra-duty patrol officers rounded up 1,453 black and Latino teenagers. By the time "Operation Hammer" was over, LAPD files listed nearly half of all black males in Los Angeles ages 21 to 24 as gang members, and every neighborhood was rife with kids who told tales of dubious arrests and petty harassment.

SOURCE. David Whitman, "The Untold Story of the LA Riot," US News & World Report, *May 23, 1993.*

other populations, as has been the case of immigrants to America. . . .

According to an idea articulated as early as 1782 and gaining currency throughout the 19th and early 20th centuries, America was destined to be a melting pot of immigrant ethnic groups, each losing its separate identity in a new blend that drew the best genetic and cultural qualities from its components. . . . The idea was so appealing to both the popular and scientific mind that contrary evidence was rarely noted. Yet, throughout our history, conspicuous divisions have persisted between blacks, Anglos, Asians, and Latinos; between Protestants, Catholics, and Jews; and between Irish, Italians, English, and other national-origin groups. The divisions are reflected in ethnic endogamy, voluntary associations, and exclusionary practices in employment, education, and housing.

> Ethnic cohesion and residential clustering . . . are most likely to cause interethnic trouble when some ethnic populations are growing locally and others are shrinking.

Ethnic cohesion and residential clustering go together; but they are most likely to cause interethnic trouble when some ethnic populations are growing locally and others are shrinking—whether because of differential vital rates, in- and out-migration, or assimilation and upward social mobility. We have pointed out how the black ghetto of South Central has been reshaped by the numerical growth and territorial expansion of Los Angeles' Latino population, and nearly surrounded by a growing population of Asians who enter the ghetto as shopkeepers but live outside the area. This pattern of ethnic pressure on residential neighborhoods, less familiar than the black-on-white pressure that prompted the "white flight" to the suburbs in the 1960s, is a source of tension in other California cities as well as in Los Angeles.

Young Males with Time on Their Hands

South Central's large pool of young males, neither steadily employed nor in school, is a pattern repeated within other California cities. The daily lives of these youths include drug and alcohol abuse and frequent criminal enterprises. Among those convicted of riot-related felonies in Los Angeles County, 60 percent had criminal records and only a third were employed. Three-fifths were high school dropouts.

> " If . . . territorially based ethnic tension is endemic in multiethnic states . . . and most cities contain a large pool of young idle males instantly available for vandalism and looting, we ought to expect more riots. "

Young males of all ethnic groups have abundant physical energy and a taste for risky enterprises. An important function of the traditional family is to restrain this energy and channel it into socially useful activities. An important function of the economic system is to provide rewarding opportunities for socially useful activities. In South Central and elsewhere, families and the economy have jointly failed in these functions, leaving young males largely unprepared for adult life and responsibilities and for serious engagement in the world of work.

Regrettably, the failures of socialization and employment opportunities reinforce each other. South Central's family structure is weakened by the inability of adults to find jobs that will support an intact family; poorly socialized young men are generally the last and most reluctantly hired, and only when labor is scarce. Most reformers pin their hopes on education and job-training by public institutions, expecting them to take over the traditional family's now-abdicated responsibilities. But even this is probably too late.

Prognosis for More Riots

If, as we contend, territorially based ethnic tension is endemic in multiethnic states such as California and most

Two young men suspected of looting are arrested in South Central Los Angeles on May 1, 1992. Some argue that high unemployment among young black people contributed to the riots. (© **AP Photo/John Gaps III.**)

cities contain a large pool of young idle males instantly available for vandalism and looting, we ought to expect more riots. We do, but only one per city.

We think that the Los Angeles riot of April 1992 could have been prevented by competently organized police action between the time of the initial disturbances and the general conflagration. To be sure, it is easy to criticize failed police tactics from the comfort of an academic armchair, but in this case it seems clear that the police command structure simply evaporated, leaving the troops in the field without guidance. The chief of police was attending a fund-raising party in Beverly Hills during the crucial hours, and none of his subordinates seemed willing to commit manpower to the trouble spots even though officers were assembled and ready for action.

Such a conspicuous breakdown usually has civic consequences. In this case, Los Angeles acquired a new police chief, and he meticulously prepared for the next likely riot flashpoint—the verdicts in the federal court trial of the police who beat Rodney King. Because two officers were found guilty of violating King's civil rights, black leaders declared a victory and there was no riot. But it was also clear that the police would respond quickly and much more effectively to street-corner disturbances this time around.

After a riot, many who participated have second thoughts. It is generally agreed that the damage inflicted by rioters to their own turf was a heavy blow to economic enterprise in South Central Los Angeles, and that it deprived the residents of access to convenient retail and financial services. Residents of South Central who did *not* riot—a clear majority—are unlikely to welcome a replay.

Incidents of interethnic violence or injustice will surely occur in the next few years, and some will result in street-corner disturbances. We doubt that these disturbances will flare again into a major riot. Before that can happen, Los Angeles must first forget what it learned this time.

Lessons from the L.A. Riot

If history carries any lessons here, they pertain to the two preconditions—ethnic tensions over territory and a critical mass of idle young men—that make areas like South Central ripe for conflagration. They are preconditions that all Californians must confront and address in the future, as the State's changing demographic complexion heightens ethnic identification with territory.

Today Los Angeles is one of only two among California's 58 counties where no single racial or ethnic group is the "majority" population. This ethnic mosaic consists of four large groups—Anglos, Hispanics, blacks, and Asians—or numerous small ones, since people actually identify themselves as Salvadorans, Filipinos, Koreans, Vietnamese, Hmong, Armenians, Iranians, and others. Typically, each group clusters residentially, often in neighborhoods that adjoin ethnically different territory.

Variants of this ethnic mosaic structure will emerge in ever more California counties during the 1990s. We estimate that 15 counties will have acquired this demographic complexion by 2010. On a statewide basis, California will have become a collection of "minorities," thereby outmoding that term. But vocabulary trails reality where local tides of immigration and assimilation wash against old neighborhood boundaries, challenging the established ethnic territory and identity. So long as ethnicity corresponds to geography, every "us" implies a "them."

Tension over turf will be a persistent feature of California's multi-ethnic society, but the tension could be peacefully managed under favorable circumstances. An important unfavorable circumstance is the presence, especially in low-income neighborhoods, of a large number of idle young males, neither steadily employed nor in school. Young males, whatever their ethnic identities, have energy and a taste for risky enterprises. Traditionally, their families have joined with schools and workplaces to restrain adventures and channel energy into gainful employment and subsequently into a recognized stake in a peaceful and safe community. All three of these institutions are visibly failing those functions, not just in South Central, but in low-income urban areas throughout the state. For those Californians who value both social justice and civil order, the prospects are bleak.

The Liberal Philosophy of Defending Black Racial Hatred Led to the Riots

Dennis Prager

In the following viewpoint, a conservative talk show host blames the 1992 Los Angeles riots on a liberal philosophy that condones racial hatred. He argues that nothing justifies the death and destruction wrought in the riots. Although rage is a universal response to frustration, he contends that moral people control this rage. Liberals foster black rage by supporting the view that the United States is a nation of racists, he contends. Liberal glorification of blacks who hate the United States essentially sends the message that the nation deserves to be burned, he argues. The fact that countries such as Germany can produce great beauty and great evil proves that nothing in highly-developed society prevents indecent acts. Thus, the author fears for the future of the United States. Dennis Prager is a syndicated radio talk show host, columnist, author, and public speaker.

SOURCE. Dennis Prager, "Liberalism and the Los Angeles Riots," Heritage Foundation, May 26, 1992. Copyright © 1992 by The Heritage Foundation. All rights reserved. Reproduced by permission.

I want to talk to you about liberalism and what happened in my city. And yes, it is my city: I don't want to be melodramatic, but just a few weeks ago the entire sky outside my house was black with smoke. If you have never had that sensation, then it is not possible for you to know exactly what it felt like. I get the chills as I tell it to you.

> Los Angeles and America were drowning in lies—most particularly that evil was not taking place.

My reaction was intense anger. I have been broadcasting on KABC, the talk radio station in Los Angeles for ten years. The station called me during the rioting and asked me if I wanted to do two live hours, even though it was not my day to broadcast. I said yes, but then my family begged me not to go—which was quite understandable since on the block of my station a FEDCO, a huge store, was being burned and looted; and next door to my station a Sees Candy was being looted (presumably because the looters had a particularly great need for candy).

Drowning in Lies

But I didn't go for another reason. I called the station and said, "I can't broadcast. I am too angry. What I have to say will not calm the city." By Saturday, I had calmed down just enough to give my commentary. My theme was that I was living in a sea of lies, that Los Angeles and America were drowning in lies—most particularly that evil was not taking place.

Let me give you one example. As I was watching the local NBC television coverage of the rioting, this is the way one reporter described what he saw: "Here I am on the corner of (I forget the streets) and I see five black gentlemen throwing stones at cars." I said on my radio show, "Can you imagine anybody ever saying, 'I saw five white gentlemen in hoods burning a cross.'?" And so, my motto—which I repeated in South Central Los Angeles to black listeners—became "If you can't call a black thug a thug, you are a racist." The inability to call a bad black person a bad person is part of the quarter-century liberal harvest. . . .

I want to dissect what liberal thought has done to America. But before I do, I need to make two things clear.

One is my own commitment to furthering black/white relationships. It is so deep that one of the reasons I founded the Micah Center for Ethical Monotheism was to combat racism through a program called "Dinners in Black and White." In it blacks and whites will simply have dinners at each others' homes—nothing else. All we want is that they have dinner with each other so that they see each other as people and not members of a race. It is one of the first three programs of my center, and it predated the rioting by months. So, I am deeply, deeply committed to eradicating racism.

Abandoning True Liberalism

My second point is that not every liberal holds every value that I am about to identify with liberalism. I understand that. Therefore, liberals hearing this should not say, "Well, I'm a liberal and I don't feel that way." I frequently hear this from callers to my radio show. I will state a liberal position and then someone will call and say, "Well I'm a liberal and I don't hold that position." So I then raise five other liberal positions, and they tell me that they don't hold them either. So I ask, "Why do you call yourself a liberal? If you don't hold these basic positions of the *New York Times* and the *Washington Post,* why do you call yourself a liberal?"

Maybe it is time for people who do not hold the positions I am about to describe, yet who call themselves liberal, to painfully acknowledge what this liberal Jew had to painfully acknowledge—that contemporary liberalism has abandoned us. Indeed, to be loyal to traditional liberal values may demand intense opposition to contemporary liberalism.

The following ideas called liberal by liberals contributed, I believe instrumentally, to what took place in Los Angeles.

Rage is all the rage. Everybody is speaking about black rage. The *L.A. Times* had a five-part series on the roots of the riots, and one of the days the entire issue was titled "Rage."

A word about rage. I would love to know if there were liberals in Germany in 1938, after *Kristallnacht* when white thugs burned Jewish establishments and killed Jews, who said, "Listen, you have to understand the rage of those Germans—they've endured the humiliating Versailles Treaty, terrible authoritarian upbringing and Germany's awful economic problems." Do you think that Nazis didn't have rage? In fact, can you name an evil in the world that is not accompanied by great rage? Do Ku Klux Klanners not have great rage? What about Jeffrey Dahmer?[1] What if somebody said, "Let's try to understand Jeffrey Dahmer's rage, and then we can really get to the roots, the underlying causes of why he murdered and ate people."

> The difference between moral people and immoral people is that moral people control their rage.

Controlling Rage

I am tired of this rage argument. It doesn't hold, and it certainly doesn't justify. And it's a tautology: all evil comes from rage. So what? The difference between moral people and immoral people is that moral people control their rage. Buddhists in Vietnam were enraged by policies of the Diem government. But they burned themselves. If the L.A. rioters had burned themselves, I would have said, "You know something? There is a real rage there which we need to listen to. These are clearly people who want to make a moral point."

But when you say, "I am enraged, so I burn others," am I supposed to listen to your rage? And what about the rage of the Koreans and blacks whose livelihoods were burned? Their rage is not discussed; it is a non-issue.

I said on my radio show right after the riots that I started to understand even better Pastor Niehmohler, the German pastor. His famous statement was essentially: "When the Nazis came after Communists I kept quiet, because I wasn't a Communist. When they came after the Jews, I said nothing, because I am not a Jew. When they came after labor leaders, I said nothing, because I am not a labor leader. And when they came after me, there was nobody left to speak up for me."

That is why we must speak up for the Koreans. I begged my fellow Jews and I begged the Los Angeles community generally, "Speak up, speak up." What happened was evil. It is not enough to say it was "rage."

And by the way, on the issue of rage, I think we are psychologically sophisticated enough to recognize that all of us have rage. What do you do at your psychoanalyst's office if not speak about your rage—at your mother, at your father, at your brother, at your sister, at your kids, at your boss, at your wife, at your husband, at life? Who doesn't have rage? So rage is universal, not an excuse for evil.

The Liberal Contribution to Rage

Let's now talk about black rage beyond the issue of whether it excuses violence. Does it really exist? Yes it does. But I hold the liberal world, black and white, very much responsible for it. I will tell you exactly why. If for thirty years all you are told is that America is racist—that whites are racist, that whites have it in for you, that no matter what you do, they are going to stomp on you—that would certainly cause a lot of rage in me if I were a black who believed it.

It would be as if I raised my Jewish children saying, "America is an antisemitic country where you can't get ahead because they hate Jews. Oh, there are token Jews here and there, but look at the absence of Jews among Fortune 500 executives, and don't think a Jew could ever be elected President; and don't forget all those country clubs that still don't allow Jews; and remember all the swastikas that are up in various places. This country hates you, my Jewish child." Gee, if nearly every Jew and non-Jew said the same thing to my children their entire lifetime, they, too, would be filled with rage. It's hard to fault blacks for their rage: The liberal media, the liberal civil rights organizations, liberal professors, and liberal artists have all told them, "You are hated. This country stinks. It is worse than ever. It has it in for you.". . .

Paul Conrad, the cartoonist of the *Los Angeles Times,* one of the best known liberal cartoonists, drew George [H.W.] Bush in a Ku Klux Klan outfit when Mr. Bush opposed the recent Civil Rights law. The point was clear: If you don't agree with us liberals on race, you are a Ku Klux Klanner. Well, if I am black and I see such cartoons often enough, what am I supposed to conclude but that this country is worthy of being burned down?

> This is my *j'accuse* to the liberal world: You have stated, in essence, that America deserves to be burned.

The Liberal Heritage

This is my *j'accuse*[2] to the liberal world: You have stated, in essence, that America deserves to be burned. That has been your reaction to Los Angeles and that was the way you portrayed America prior to it. We deserve to be burned, and the burners need to be heard. That is the liberal heritage that we have received over all these years.

Liberals respond to this by saying, "We love our country, and we express this love by criticizing it." I think

that Irving Kristol [a neoconservative writer] answered that best: What would you say about a husband or wife who constantly spoke about how awful his or her spouse was? Would you be impressed by the person's defense, "Oh, I just criticize the person I love"?

At a given point the issue whether you love in your heart or not is irrelevant; your actions are what matter. And liberal actions—I don't care about liberal motives, I am sure they are pure—have said this country is worthy of burning.

The burning has happened, and it probably will happen again, because the official American media and liberal political reaction has been: "Arsonists, we understand you." We had a United States Representative, Maxine

A demonstrator burns a US flag at a protest against the Rodney King trial verdict, in front of the headquarters of the Los Angeles police department on April 30, 1992. (© **AP Photo/Nick Ut.**)

Waters, screaming, "No justice, no peace." In other words, "Do what we want, or we will burn you." Think of that—a member of the U.S. House of Representatives at a rally in Washington led the chant, "Give us what we want or we will burn you." In other words, until then, you deserve to be burned. That has been the liberal message.

The Liberal Indictment of the United States

With all of this teaching of America's perfidy, no wonder there is a lot of black rage. No wonder about twenty percent of blacks, and according to one poll, twenty-nine percent, believe that whites started AIDS in order to commit genocide against blacks. It makes sense. Since this is such an awful country, maybe it's true.

If you think that this depiction of the liberal indictment of America is in any way exaggerated, let me read to you just a few of mainstream liberal comments on the riots.

One of the chief liberal spokespeople on this has been Andrew Hacker, whose recent book, *Two Nations Black and White: Separate, Hostile and Equal,* has been virtually beatified by the liberal press. This is what he wrote in the *Los Angeles Times* on May 13th [1992]:

> So there is the sheer strain of living in a white world, the rage that you must suppress almost every day. . . . The conclusion seems all but self-evident that white America has no desire for your presence or any need for your people. Can this nation have an unstated strategy for annihilating your people?

Whites want to annihilate you, black Americans. That comes from a leading liberal academic in a leading liberal newspaper in the city of the riots two weeks after they occurred.

Walter Mosely, a black author of *Devil in a Blue Dress,* or *Red Death,* and other mysteries that are set in Los

Angeles, wrote in the *Los Angeles Times,* May 5, 1992: "America is a brutal land. Its language is violence and bloodshed. That is why [Rodney] King was beaten; that is why another [Martin Luther] King was assassinated."

There's the liberal message: America, not one despicable racist, murdered Dr. King.

I'll give you another example. Leon Litwack, the A.F. and May T. Morrison Professor of American History at UC Berkeley, wrote in the *Los Angeles Times,* May 5, 1992: "The lawlessness began with the clubbing of black America, the conscious and criminal neglect and fashionable racism characteristic of the Age of Greed, over which Ronald Reagan and George Bush have presided."

> For thirty years, liberals have glorified blacks who hate America.

That is a distinguished professor of history at Berkeley teaching how this country clubs blacks, has fashionable racism, and is filled with criminals in its establishment. How would you react if you were one of his black students?

That is what has set the agenda for all of what has happened. For thirty years, liberals have glorified blacks who hate America—from the day that the late Leonard Bernstein threw a party at his Park Avenue penthouse for the Black Panthers [a black revolutionary organization]. Do you understand what announcement was being made? The elite of America only honor blacks who loathe America—the more you hate America, the more the white elite will honor you. If you are a black and you say you love this country, we have only contempt for you. You are an Uncle Tom[3]; you are worse, you are an inauthentic black. But if you truly loathe America, if you truly believe that it is a despicable place, then we will honor you—you will get to the cover of *Time;* you will get the support of major liberal foundations. You are the ones we will hear.

This message has not changed since Leonard Bernstein threw that party. If you are a black who says, "This country is wonderful. Sure it has got racists in it, but it is wonderful, and we have opportunities," you are loathed. A man named Clarence Thomas [who was confirmed as a US Supreme Court justice on October 23, 1991] is the classic example. The day he thanked nuns and his grandparents, I knew he was dead. That was the death knell. What—nuns? A black thanking normative, Judaeo-Christian religion? That has to be silenced. And every effort other than actual murder was used. There was, of course, the attempted murder of a name, which, incidentally, Judaism considers morally equivalent to murder. There is a statement in Hebrew, "He who insults his neighbor in public, it is as if he has spilled his blood." Clarence Thomas had the temerity to say, "This is a good country." And when a black says that, he is in big trouble with white and black liberals. . . .

The Fragility of Civilization

I conclude by noting that there is a profound naiveté on the part of liberals with regard to the fragility of civilization. I stand here as a Jew who is too well aware of this fragility. The country that gave us [composer Johann Sebastian] Bach, [composer Ludwig van] Beethoven, and [writer Friedrich] Schiller gave us Auschwitz [a Nazi concentration camp]. To my mind, it is not at all contradictory, because there is nothing whatsoever in art and culture that demands decency—nothing. No matter how highly developed they are, it does not matter morally. There truly is a thin line between what we have created in America and the possibilities of an Auschwitz or a Gulag [a system of forced labor camps in the Soviet Union]. And those who do not recognize this, who think that civilization can take a beating—that liberal democratic civilization can constantly be beaten and called, in effect, fascistic—are weakening this civilization, perhaps fatally.

Historian Walter Lacquer, writing about the Left in the Weimar Republic, wrote, and I paraphrase: "They kept calling the judges and the police and the institutions of the Weimar Republic fascist. One day they met real fascists And they had nothing left to call them." You can scream and scream about how racist, sexist, oppressive, and callous America is—but there are just so many such body blows that America can take. It has been taking the liberals' body blows and it is now down for a count. The smoke rising by my home a few weeks ago made me aware of that. I fear for this country. It is the first time in my life I fear for this country. People who say they love it are giving it body blows. And, tragically, they are called liberals.

> There are only two races in this world . . . the decent and the indecent.

There are only two races in this world, the eminent psychoanalyst Victor Frankl concluded after going through Auschwitz—the decent and the indecent. That is the only thing that we need to know, and it is the single most important teaching being undermined by liberalism in our time.

Notes:

1. Jeffrey Dahmer was a US serial killer and sex offender who committed the rape, murder, and dismemberment of seventeen men and boys between 1978 and 1991.
2. *J'accuse* was an inflammatory open letter from writer Émile Zola that was published in the newspaper *L'Aurore* in 1898.
3. An Uncle Tom is a black man who will do anything to stay in good standing with white people, including betray his own people.

Denouncement of the Rodney King Police Brutality Verdict Prompted the Riots

Scott Holleran

Written on the twentieth anniversary of the 1992 Los Angeles riots, the following viewpoint asserts that official denouncement of the Rodney King verdict was the riot's actual cause. A journalist maintains that the jury, which came to its decision based on the facts rather than on biased media reports, rightly concluded that the police officers accused of police brutality had no intent to violate King's rights. Nevertheless, respected public figures such as Los Angeles mayor Tom Bradley denounced the verdict rather than urge calm and acceptance. President George H.W. Bush also denounced the verdict, in effect challenging the legitimacy of a legal ruling. The media bombarded the public with the message

SOURCE. Scott Holleran, "Remembering the 1992 Los Angeles Riots," *Capitalism Magazine,* April 27, 2012. Copyright © 2012 by Scott Holleran. All rights reserved. Reproduced by permission.

that the verdict was a racist conspiracy. Thus, the author maintains, the violence was no surprise—a clear lesson of what can happen when government officials engage in race-baiting rather than promote public safety. Scott Holleran is a journalist who has written for the *Philadelphia Inquirer, Los Angeles Times,* and *Wall Street Journal.*

This week [April 2012] marks the 20th anniversary of L.A.'s riots. They were sparked by a mixed verdict in a racially-charged trial of four police officers accused of using excessive force against a suspect. His name was Rodney King. He had refused to cooperate in an arrest that was being videotaped which would be broadcast nationwide.

April 29, 1992, was a horrible day in Los Angeles. Within a week, 53 were killed, 2,000 were injured, $1 billion in property was lost and the city was looted and burned for days, while people and businesses were targeted for attack based on race until U.S. Armed Forces were dispatched and citywide curfews were imposed.

What caused the riots began to unfold on March 3, 1991, when paroled felon Rodney King, who is black, led police on a high-speed chase through streets and freeways, ending in an arrest that the 6-foot, 3-inch King resisted while intoxicated. King was severely beaten by four non-black police officers that were being filmed on amateur video without their knowledge. The video was released to the press, causing charges of police brutality and racism in a police department with a track record of racism. Amid the uproar, King was soon released and, instead, the officers were charged with a crime (assault with a deadly weapon and excessive use of force, among other charges). A jury trial ensued and the 12-member jury came back with a not guilty verdict on all counts except one. Few who had followed the facts of the case were surprised. The prosecution had been required to

Los Angeles Mayor Tom Bradley

The first African American mayor of Los Angeles, Tom Bradley (1917–1998) won election five times, serving a record 20 years in a city where African Americans constituted a small minority of the electorate. . . .

Bradley joined the Los Angeles police force for what turned into a 21-year career (1940–1961) and rose through the ranks to lieutenant. In the 1950s Bradley enrolled in night school and completed his law studies at Southwestern University, where he received an LL.B. [undergraduate law] degree in 1956 and won admission to the California bar the next year. . . . After his police career, Bradley practiced law briefly and in 1963

won a seat as Los Angeles' first African American city councilman. . . .

Bradley won a stunning upset [against the incumbent mayor in 1973], carrying 56 percent of the vote in a city in which African Americans comprised only 15 percent of the electorate. Bradley won reelection four times, several of those with even larger majorities. He carried 59 percent of the vote in 1977, 64 percent in 1981, and 67 percent in 1985, achieving a precedent-setting fourth term. . . .

Bradley's later administration was marred by conflict and scandal, largely as a result of the Rodney King incident and the riots that ensued when the involved officers were acquitted. On

show that the officers *intended* to violate King's rights by beating him. Most trial reporters indicated that no such intent had been demonstrated.

Challenging the Legitimacy of the Verdict

So, what caused the worst American riot of the 20th century?

As the highly publicized case went to court, with biased reports, partial airings and frame-by-frame photographs of the video omitting relevant facts, Los Angeles Mayor Tom Bradley urged Los Angeles Police Chief Darryl Gates to resign. Chief Gates in turn refused to quit and launched a public campaign to keep his job. Both did this while the case was being adjudicated. Their public

March 3, 1991, King was severely beaten by Los Angeles police officers, and the event was recorded on videotape. Four officers were charged with assault and controversial police chief Darryl Gates was suspended, then reinstated. Mayor Bradley urged Gates to resign, and when he refused, communication between the two disintegrated. A year later, when the verdict in the officers' trial sparked riots in South Central Los Angeles, Gates was again at the center of the controversy. A panel led by former FBI and CIA director William Webster held Gates responsible for not having an adequate plan to deal with potential unrest. But Webster also blamed Mayor Bradley for poor rela-tions between the police department and city hall. Bradley confessed that he and Gates had not spoken for over a year before the riots. The riots had a devastating impact on the city and on Bradley's administration. . . .

He died of a heart attack on September 29, 1998. A reserved man who was known as a hardworking and conscientious administrator, Tom Bradley was among the leading African American political figures in the United States.

SOURCE. *"Bradley, Tom (1917–1998),"* Encyclopedia of World Biography. *Gale, 1998. Copyright © 1998 by Cengage Learning.*

battle divided the city, raising the stakes and inhibiting the city's ability to handle any crisis.

Mayor Bradley denounced the jury's verdict before urging acceptance. The police chief obstinately refused to respond on the first day of rioting, issuing statements that police were responding despite reports to the contrary—in Koreatown, merchants under gunfire were forced into protracted battles to save their lives and property—while Chief Gates attended a fund-raiser. Most deserving of blame, however, is the president: George Herbert Walker Bush. Immediately after the verdict was announced, Bush issued the following denunciation of the verdict:

> Viewed from outside the trial, it was hard to understand
> how the verdict could possibly square with the video.

US president George H.W. Bush (second from left) tours riot-torn areas of Los Angeles in May 1992. Some argue that the deep sense of unaddressed injustice felt by US minorities was validated by the strong condemnation of the verdict in the Rodney King trial by important figures such as President Bush. (© Diana Walker/ Time Life Pictures/Getty Images.)

Those civil rights leaders with whom I met were stunned. And so was I and so was Barbara and so were my kids.

For an American president to denounce a verdict in a case that had been given due process was bad enough. Bush's comments challenged the legitimacy of a proper legal ruling. The media, which had half-reported on the case without regard to crucial facts, shares blame, but the first ex-President Bush is at least partly responsible for the blood spilled in Los Angeles.

Bombarded by Distorted Media Messages

In fact, by the time news of the verdict spread, the people of Los Angeles had essentially been bombarded with the message from the media, the mayor and the president that Rodney King (who has since been arrested 11 times) was a victim of a racist police conspiracy and that any claim to the contrary was either outrageous or itself evidence of racism. So it was not surprising when white truck driver Reginald Denny was pulled out of his truck and nearly beaten to death by a gang of predominantly black thugs (Denny was saved by a black man, as were other victims on that day of death and destruction).

> " The first ex-President Bush is at least partly responsible for the blood spilled in Los Angeles. "

Seeing Reginald Denny being assaulted and mutilated for the color of his skin on live television provided an unforgettable lesson in the politics of race-baiting: that jumping to conclusions may impair government from protecting the public and instead incur looting and killing. L.A.'s riots are a harsh reminder that replacing facts with feelings—which was done by city leaders, the president and a pack of journalists—is a matter of life and death.

The Los Angeles Police Department Failed to Protect Local Citizens During the Riots

Jim Newton

During the early hours of the 1992 Los Angeles riots, the media noted the conspicuous absence of the police. In the following viewpoint, a veteran of the *Los Angeles Times* argues twenty years later that the LAPD failed in its duty to protect and serve. Before the riots, the LAPD relied on harsh and coercive law enforcement tactics. However, when violence erupted following the Rodney King verdict, the LAPD was clearly absent. In fact, Police Chief Daryl Gates was at a fundraiser to defeat a proposal requiring LAPD reforms. When a commission established to investigate the LAPD's performance during the riots expressed serious concern about the department's lack of readiness, Gates's response reflected the callous and unsympathetic tactics he advocated. Jim Newton, who

SOURCE. Jim Newton, "The Night the LAPD Failed," *Los Angeles Times,* April 29, 2012. Copyright © 2012. Los Angeles Times. Reprinted with permission.

has worked as a reporter, editor, and bureau chief, is now editor at large of the *Los Angeles Times*.

T he Los Angeles riots represented the culmination of many failures: the failure to provide hope for young people; the failure to supply education and jobs in the numbers that would stabilize communities; the failure to engage those communities in their own protection instead of relying on harsh and coercive law enforcement.

Failing to Protect and Serve

But on the night of April 29, 1992, 20 years ago today, the overriding failure was that of the Los Angeles Police Department and its chief, Daryl F. Gates. The LAPD has a civic duty "to protect and to serve"; that night, it did neither.

> The LAPD has a civic duty "to protect and to serve"; that night, it did neither.

I witnessed that lapse firsthand. On the afternoon that the verdicts were read in Simi Valley, my colleague Rick Serrano, who covered the LAPD, was in the court-room. I was a 29-year-old reporter newly assigned to the paper's downtown newsroom. Because Serrano was tied up, I was asked to spend the afternoon at Parker Center, the headquarters of the LAPD, and to record the reaction to the verdicts.

They were announced in mid-afternoon, and most of the officers I saw seemed subdued. A few pumped fists or quietly expressed satisfaction that the jury had sided with their colleagues, but there were no celebrations or exultation—at least in front of a reporter.

Outside, by contrast, there was shock and dismay. It was a hot day, and on the streets of what was then still called South-Central, anger swelled in the heat.

The Florence and Normandie Intersection Was the Flashpoint of the Riots

No one noticed [Los Angeles Police Chief] Daryl Gates as he was driven north to Brentwood on the San Diego Freeway, following the route that O.J. Simpson would take two years later in the famous slow-speed chase that ended in his arrest. On April 29, 1992, the eyes of the world were focused on the bloody intersection of Florence and Normandie, where in the wake of the LAPD's withdrawal a gang-led mob took control and attacked anyone who was not African American. Because the police had failed to seal off this well-traveled route through South Central, targets were plentiful. Whites, Asians, and Latinos were hauled from vehicles and beaten or attacked on the streets. Most of the victims were poor, small, or frail. None had any connection with the LAPD or Rodney King.

These racially charged assaults were recorded by television cameras on news helicopters hovering over the intersection as horrified pilots added commentary. "And there's no police presence down here!" an observer in one helicopter said at the height of the violence. "They will not enter the area. This is attempted murder! Tell LAPD to shut Florence Boulevard down, and Normandie."

While the savagery at Florence and Normandie was witnessed by the nation live on television, it was not seen by the mayor, the police chief, or many high-ranking LAPD officers. . . .

In the aftermath of the riots, Gates would complain that television coverage distorted what happened in South Central after the verdicts. He disputed the notion that Florence and Normandie was the "flash point" of the riots, saying that the media focus on the intersection obscured "outbreaks of violence" that occurred over thirty square miles of South Central. Defending himself against the charge that abandonment of the site had set the riots in motion, Gates offered the excuse that LAPD officers had been preoccupied with too many calls to focus on a single intersection.

That self-serving argument was inconsistent with the chief's criticism of [Lieutenant Mike] Moulin, who Gates said had sent the wrong message when he did not try to retake Florence and Normandie. The reason the message was important was that Florence and Normandie at the time was the focus of violence in South Central, not simply one incident among many. This is clear from the well-documented analysis of the riot's first six hours prepared at Gates' behest by the LAPD's Inspection and Control Section. This report dutifully repeats the chief's assertion that "the media declared" Florence and Normandie the flash point of the riots. But it goes on to show that the declaration was accurate.

SOURCE. Lou Cannon, *Official Negligence. New York: Random House, 1997, pp. 303, 306.*

People who had gathered in the expectation of seeing officers punished for a brutal beating instead saw them vindicated.

Late that afternoon, when a group of young men at Florence and Normandie beat Reginald Denny to a pulp, smashing his head with a brick, police held back.

Unwilling to Risk Confrontation

The message seemed fairly clear: The LAPD, so long accused of brutality, on this night was unwilling to risk confrontation. Outside Parker Center, a growing mob gathered in the hours after the verdict and taunted the police inside. I stood beside two members of the Police Commission as rocks and chunks of concrete began to pelt the building. Officers fingered their weapons nervously but did not respond. It was not their fault: Warned not to confront the angry crowd and equipped with no other plan, they waited for orders that did not come.

> The LAPD, so long accused of brutality, on this night was unwilling to risk confrontation.

Gates, who had not spoken to Mayor Tom Bradley in more than a year, had left headquarters to attend a gathering in Brentwood to raise money for defeating proposed reforms of his department. As the violence outside his office escalated, Gates was unreachable. Protesters turned over a guard shack and set it on fire. Police watched.

I recently was given a photograph of that police guard shack on fire. In the picture, I'm on the edge of the crowd, taking notes, a conspicuously white guy with a necktie, lit by firelight. There is not a police officer to be seen. Gates later accused me of lacking standing to criticize the department's performance on April 29. In fact, I was there; he wasn't.

In the grand, violent history of Los Angeles, there are plenty of moments inspired by greed and vengeance and

Los Angeles police chief Daryl Gates talks to reporters on May 1, 1992, about the riots. He was blamed by critics for the police department's failure during the beginning of the riots and was replaced soon therafter. (© Douglas Burrows/Liaison/Hulton Archive/Getty Images.)

lust; there are, in addition, two monumental personal failures: William Mulholland's tragic miscalculation at the St. Francis Dam that led to its collapse in 1928, killing hundreds and shattering the great engineer's reputation, and Gates' absence on April 29, 1992.

The Tragic End to Gates's Career

Analyzing the LAPD's performance that night and in the chaotic days that followed, a commission chaired by William Webster, the former director of the FBI and CIA, concluded that the department's lack of readiness was a "cause for grave concern" and warranted a substantial overhaul of the LAPD. Gates was forced from his job, and his successors remade the department.

It was, for Gates, the tragic end to a mixed career. In his heyday, he was regarded as one of the LAPD's finest staff officers (many consider him the greatest deputy chief in the LAPD's history). And he was an honest, devoted public servant who gave much to this city. But he also was a reckless blowhard who deliberately antagonized many well-meaning residents and abandoned his post at the moment leadership was most required.

Then again, there is the question of what he might have done if he had been in his office that evening rather than politicking across town. After the Webster report was released, here was Gates's response: "Clearly that night we should have gone down there and shot a few people. In retrospect, that's exactly what we should have done. We should have blown a few heads off."

The Mainstream Media Failed to Report the Conditions That Led to the Riots

Harold Jackson

Although the violence, arson, and looting in the 1992 Los Angeles riots generally shocked white people, the riots only dismayed black people familiar with the conditions in South Central Los Angeles, claims a black journalist in the following viewpoint. The media failure to report the daily carnage that occurs in US inner cities easily explains white America's surprise, the author contends. Rather than consult rap artists whose hateful lyrics advocate violence as a solution to frustration and despair, the media instead interviewed black leaders out of touch with the streets. While the media often reports statistics about violence, it rarely gives the reader perspective, the author maintains. To be trusted to tell the whole story, the author asserts that the media must share the stories of

SOURCE. Harold Jackson, "We Weren't Listening," *Nieman Reports,* Winter–Spring 1999–2000, pp. 151–152. Copyright © 1999 by Nieman Reports. All rights reserved. Reproduced by permission.

the young people in these communities who feel they do not matter. Harold Jackson is a Pulitzer Prize–winning journalist who has written for the *Birmingham News,* the *Baltimore Sun,* and is now the editorial page editor of the *Philadelphia Inquirer.*

Conversations with blacks and whites during the three days of mayhem that followed the April 29 [1992] verdicts in the Rodney King police beating case revealed a difference of opinion that pollsters were late to record.

While whites were shocked and appalled at the assaults, the looting, the firebombings, many blacks were only appalled. The subtle difference is that a lot of blacks weren't really surprised at the violent reaction to the innocent verdicts given the cops accused of beating King.

> That most whites had not previously realized the degree of rage among black youths that exploded in the Los Angeles riots can in part be attributed to the media's ineptness.

That most whites had not previously realized the degree of rage among black youths that exploded in the Los Angeles riot can in part be attributed to the media's ineptness in reporting why that rage existed. It didn't start with the Rodney King case.

White readers, watchers and listeners of the daily news absorb the fact that homicide has become the leading cause of death among young black men as easily as they wipe up a kitchen counter spill with a Bounty towel. The media have failed to provide them with the perspective to be genuinely touched by such numbers.

Failing to Report Urban Carnage

The carnage occurring in America's cities daily is not normal; rage is its fuel. But because of the way it is reported, as news from the urban war front, far removed from where they live, many whites simply don't care to know why the people involved are killing each other. They don't know them.

Even black suburbanites, however, can't help identifying with what is happening in the inner cities. Many of them came from such surroundings. Some have personally witnessed the disregard for human life that would allow someone to uncaringly shoot anyone within range of a speeding car or stomp on the head of another human being.

The media daily provide glimpses of such aberrant behavior, but those glimpses were not enough to prepare TV-watching white America for the sight of Reginald Denny being pulled from his truck, beaten bloody, then shot in the leg.

Perhaps white America would not have been as surprised had the media done better reporting the messages being sent to black youths, messages that tell them violence is an acceptable means of expression.

It was almost comical to see news staffs across the country tap the usual suspects, the "black leaders," to explain the anger expressed not just in Los Angeles but in many cities from San Francisco to Atlanta.

These black leaders, usually men, usually 50-plus years of age, could relate to what was happening in the streets but they did not have the perspective of the young people participating in spontaneous anarchy.

Relating Outdated Perspectives

Why didn't the media go to today's leaders whose messages more closely resemble Bobby Seale's[1] than Martin King's, the leaders whose messages have made violent reaction the chosen form of protest among many young blacks? Why didn't they go to the rap music artists?

It is a mistake for mainstream, white media to write off this music form as sheer entertainment, totally frivolous. Rap is often political, it is often philosophical, many

of its artists have the power to motivate masses of people. In fact, some do just that.

O'Shea Jackson, the rap artist who calls himself Ice Cube, released a song last year [1991] titled "Death Certificate," that included the words "Oriental one-penny motherf---ers. . . . Pay respect to the black fist/Or we'll burn your store right down to a crisp."

Was that not the attitude of blacks who sacked Korean shops in Los Angeles? Their anger was not just jealousy that Korean merchants were doing well in black neighborhoods. They believe the Korean merchants only see blacks as customers or robbers, never as people. . . .

Some listened to the electrically charged rap of Ice Cube or other proponents of violence as a solution, artists such as N.W.A., Sister Souljah and Public Enemy,

A TV show crew member reads the newspaper while he and hundreds of reporters await the verdict in the federal trial against the officers in the Rodney King case. The media have been blamed for not adequately presenting the issues involved in the 1992 Los Angeles riots. (© AP Photo/Bob Galbraith.)

whose "By the Time I Get to Arizona" video depicts Arizona public officials being killed for opposing a Martin Luther King state holiday. News reports about Ice Cube's "Death Certificate" and Public Enemy's "By the Time I Get to Arizona" primarily concerned white reactions or the artists' defense of their work. Left unexplored was the racial climate, the anger among black youths, that would make it profitable for record companies to promote songs with those subjects.

Painting with a Stereotypical Brush

The media usually find it convenient to paint rap artists with the same stereotypical brush they use for many things African American in nature. They want to place them in a niche that does not take into account their complexities.

Reporters need to point out that artists such as Sister Souljah (Lisa Williamson) are more political activists than rap stars. A former member of Public Enemy, Sister Souljah makes fiery speeches that reflect her being both streetwise and formally educated. She spent four years at Rutgers University, with overseas studying stints in Spain, Zimbabwe and the Soviet Union. . . .

> [The media] occasionally report on the violence found in rap music, but rarely do those reports take into consideration the conditions that have created an audience for this vitriol.

Whites might not have been as surprised by the violent reaction to the King beating verdict had the media given them more than occasional disjointed reports on the violence that has so consumed the lives of many young black people that it even includes their preferred music.

The media don't hesitate to report the results of that violence, someone being maimed or murdered. They even occasionally report on the violence found in rap music, but rarely do those reports take into consideration

the conditions that have created an audience for this vit-
riol to a hip-hop beat.

Some might argue that every time there is a new re-
lease of statistics showing the depths to which America's
black citizens are still assigned, the media report it. Indeed, they have reported that black unemployment, at
more than 15 percent, is twice the rate of whites; that
blacks make up 12 percent of the U.S. workforce, but
27 percent of the chronically unemployed; that nearly
one in four black men aged 20 to 29 is either in prison
or on parole or probation; that the median household in-
come for black families is $20,000 compared to $36,000
for whites.

Missing Stories

Numbers and more numbers are reported and reported.
But what is lacking in the analytical stories that accom-
pany the statistics is the perspective that makes people
realize what those numbers say about how people feel
about themselves and others.

Missing are enough stories about the people in those
statistics that have nothing to do with numbers, positive
stories that make the reader or listener feel empathy for
that person when the statistics are released.

In retrospect, the King beating case verdict should
not have been unexpected. It is very difficult to get
people who feel this country has given up too much to
criminals to punish their protection against crime. . . .

A jury would not convict police officers of brutality
in the case of Don Jackson, the private investigator who
videotaped his arrest three years ago in Long Beach,
California. The police pushed his head through a plate
glass window. And the *Chicago Tribune* reported during
the Los Angeles riots that only six cops there have been
charged with abuse in the last 10 years and only one was
convicted, an officer who shot an unarmed man in the
back of the head during a 1983 traffic stop.

But just as the King beating trial verdict might have been expected, especially given the change of venue to a suburb popular with police retirees, the aftermath of the verdict should have been anticipated, too.

And perhaps it would have been had the media done a better job of connecting the dots, a better job of reporting that the violence being played out in urban neighborhoods daily is not just about dope deals and domestic arguments.

This violence has at its roots not just criminality but a common despair, a common belief that the system only responds to anger. That anger exists in this country wherever there are people who feel they don't count, that they are not being treated fairly, that they are not being heard. If the media doesn't listen to them and report what they are saying, then who will?

> The media are no longer trusted to tell the whole story of the neglected communities where violence is most likely to occur.

The 1960s riots saw the number of black reporters and photographers rise in cities where the media found a brown face could go where a white one could not. But the violence that broke out in cities after the King beating verdict included attacks on journalists regardless of their color.

The media are no longer trusted to tell the whole story of the neglected communities where violence is most likely to occur. The media must regain that trust.

Note:

1. Bobby Seale is a US political activist known for cofounding the Black Panther Party with Huey Newton.

The Media Misrepresented the Korean-American Story During the Riots

Dennis Romero

In the following viewpoint, a journalist shares the story of a fellow journalist and longtime friend, John Lee. At the time of the 1992 Los Angeles riots, Lee wrote for the *Los Angeles Times*. Bitter about the media portrayal of Korean Americans during the riots, he left the paper shortly after. Lee claims that the Los Angeles Police Department capitalized on the bad blood between Korean merchants and African Americans in South Los Angeles to deflect attention from the Rodney King beating. When African American teen Latasha Harlins was shot by Korean shop owner, Soon Ja Du, the police released a video of the incident that the media edited to focus on the shooting rather than the fact that Harlins had punched

SOURCE. Dennis Romero, "LA Riots: LAPD Tried to Displace Its Racism Problem and 'Put It on a Korean Merchant,' Says Former *Times* Reporter John Lee," *LA Weekly,* April 26, 2012. First published in LA Weekly, a Voice Media Group publication. Copyright © 2012 by Voice Media Group. All rights reserved. Reproduced by publication.

Du in the face several times. Du was convicted of manslaughter but was sentenced to probation, fueling rage against Korean shopkeepers during the riots. Lee also expressed disgust at the way the media painted Korean shop owners who armed themselves to defend their stores. Even years later, following the federal trial of the four police officers, the media focused on Koreans who armed themselves but not on those who wanted to avoid confrontation. Dennis Romero is a journalist who has written for the *Los Angeles Weekly*.

The riots that were sparked on April 29, 1992 put L.A.'s burgeoning Korean American population in the spotlight.

It seems that for every generation, a group of immigrants gets picked for no-holds-barred hatred, and Koreans in 1992 were it. John Lee covered the community and the riots for the *Los Angeles Times* back then, and he argues that the LAPD [Los Angeles Police Department], under fire for the Rodney King beating, wanted the focus to be on his people.

Another Spark for the Riots

Shortly after the uprisings, Lee, a longtime friend of this reporter, left the paper, bitter about his experience. He looks back. . . .

Some have forgotten that another spark for the riots was the shooting of 15-year-old Latasha Harlins less than two weeks after the police beating of King.

A South L.A. store owner, Soon Ja Du, pulled the trigger. It was March 16, 1991.

Lee covered the aftermath of the shooting and the ensuing manslaughter prosecution of Du, who claimed self defense. The storyline often cited was that Harlins was shot over a $1.79 bottle of orange juice she had stuffed in her backpack.

He interviewed Latasha's aunt, Denise Harlins, who raised her. "She dealt with me as human being and not as a Korean *L.A. Times* reporter," Lee says.

Latasha Harlins quickly became the Trayvon Martin of her day. Orange juice was her Skittles.

Harlins, it turned out, intended to pay for the juice, and died with $2 in her hand after scuffling with Du and being shot in the back of the head as she attempted to leave the store.

The Korean's family gave security video to the LAPD, hoping it would vindicate Du. But the department instead released it to the media. Lee thinks that the LAPD was trying to deflect attention away from another video—that of King being pummeled by four cops.

Capitalizing on Bad Blood

There was already bad blood in the black community: African Americans felt they were treated badly by a wave of Korean merchants that had come into South L.A. to open liquor stores, markets, clothing boutiques and wig shops. Lee was assigned to cover the Harlins story with African American colleague Andrea Ford:

> I had had that conversation with Andrea, about how Korean merchants treated black customers. We were aware of the climate. There were a lot of incidents of disputes.

He thinks the LAPD capitalized on this:

> My concern was that we were taking wholesale what the police were feeding the media through this very calculated press conference [Monday after the weekend shooting]. The calculation was to take away from the Rodney King incident and to displace their racist beating—to displace some of that shock of the racism—and put it on a Korean merchant.
>
> Korean merchants were already walking a fine line of being characterized as oppressors to African American clientele.

That day the department called for "Murder One"—a premeditated homicide charge—against Du, which Lee says was extraordinary because cops aren't responsible for bringing charges; the District Attorney's office is.

What followed, he says, was coverage that focused on the shooting of an unarmed black girl and not what happened before the gun went off.

Lee says that after police released the videotape, many news outlets edited it to show only the shooting.

Harlins actually punched Du two or three times in the face after the store owner grabbed her backpack and demanded payment for the juice that was hidden away in her bag.

Du's family contended that the weapon had been stolen and recovered and was modified, unbeknownst to the merchant, to have a hair trigger, a fact that cops seemed to corroborate.

The Impact of Media Simplification

But the story line didn't change much. It was an unprovoked shooting by a racist Korean store owner over a $1.79 bottle of juice. People were pissed and, Lee says, coverage of the incident didn't help:

> The portrayal of how Latasha Harlins was killed and how the trial went down contributed to people's righteous indignation and fueled a lot of [riot] violence directed at Korean merchants.

It was probably the incident that fueled people's anger in wanting some retribution. I feel that retribution was taken out on Korean merchants. The *Times* I think had a part in it. This case was put on this Korean family who barely spoke English and were not in a good position to defend themselves.

In November 1991 Du was convicted of manslaughter, but a judge sentenced her to probation: No time would be served. Lee:

I do feel like the portrayal of how Latasha Harlins was killed and how the trial went down contributed to people's righteous indignation and fueled a lot of [riot] violence directed at Korean merchants. The way the media simplifies things, it was pointing an arrow at Korean merchants. Whatever grievance you have with the justice system, this is your enemy. Here's your target.

When the riots erupted on April 29, some people burned Korean stores in the name of Latasha Harlins, the case still fresh in the minds of many in South L.A.

Calling Up Minority Journalists

By that time Lee had been reassigned to the San Diego edition of the *Los Angeles Times,* but soon enough, as one of only a few Korean American reporters at the paper, he was called up to cover the uprisings.

The paper had a system of suburban satellite editions in places like San Diego, Orange County, Ventura County, the Westside and the San Fernando Valley.

While some of the best journalists ever to work at the *Times* (author Michael Connelly, former *Weekly* editor Drex Heikes, national correspondent and sometime overseas reporter John Glionna) came out of the 'burbs, they were also known as the place where young minorities got their feet in the door.

And thus, when the riots happened, the paper, severely lacking minorities based out of its downtown Metro section, "called up" all the people of color it could get, even if they didn't know much about South L.A.

In a surreal twist that rings true for almost anyone who remembers the savage beauty of that warm spring, Lee, a San Diego native, says he had gone surfing the day the riots started.

I caught perfect south Bird [Rock], 4–6 feet northwest swell. Definitely probably one of the best days ever surfing that spot. It was a total trip to leave my hometown. I went from paradise to palm trees on fire.

Soon Ja Du (left) leaves court with her husband, Billy Hong Ki Du, in November 1992. She was convicted of manslaughter in the killing of Latasha Harlins in her convenience store and was sentenced to probation. (© **AP Photo/ Chris Martinez.**)

He says he drove up from San Diego that week with an African American colleague:

She was not from L.A. or Southern California. They didn't call her up for her experience or knowledge of the area. It was because she was African American.

Back then there were very few reporters on the city desk who spent any time in South L.A. A lot of them didn't know that Florence was an east-west street. It gave rise to this criticism that they were bringing in reporters from the 'burbs who would have better access to the riot areas.

An Unfair Portrayal

As he was deployed to Koreatown, Lee says the media's story was once again off.

Korean store owners were portrayed as almost feral in their armed plight to save their merchandise, he says: They had itchy trigger fingers and would shoot those who trespassed.

Often untold, however, was the fact that rioters would drive up to Korean American stores and open fire with automatic weapons. It happened at the BiF furniture store at Vermont Avenue and 8th Street, he says, a place he witnessed as it was fortified with refrigerators to create foxholes.

Also untold: Those Koreans who laid down their weapons, locked up their stores, and tried to avoid violence.

A year after the riots, Lee had left the *Times* and was working at *LA Weekly* while freelancing for the *New York Times*.

The second trial, this one federal, of the four officers in the King beating had been underway, and the story line was that Korean Americans were once again arming themselves to prepare for the worst.

> Often untold . . . was the fact that rioters would drive up to Korean American stores and open fire with automatic weapons.

The media descended on the one licensed gun seller in Koreatown, Western Guns, noting that a dozen or more weapons were heading out the door on a good day, Lee says. The image there was of an emboldened, macho Korean merchant class ready for battle once more. But a gun shop on the Westside was selling more than 150 weapons a day.

Lee interviewed a merchant who decided to downscale his merchandise to 99-cent-store-style items, leave his guns at home, and lock up. There would be no armed confrontation this time.

He was like, if people want to loot it, that's on them, and I'm not going to lose my life over it—and I'm not going to take somebody's life over it. That nuance was never covered in any other place. I tried to get that story out there.

Lee says he sent 250 inches of printed notes to the *New York Times* for its riot anniversary story, including facts about the Westside gun store and the store owner who was choosing peace.

"They ended up doing their own story," Lee says, exasperated. "They went to Western Guns."

CHAPTER 3

Personal Narratives

An Editor Explains How the *Los Angeles Times* Covered the Riots in the Midst of the Violence

Shelby Coffey III

In the following viewpoint, then *Los Angeles Times* editor Shelby Coffey III describes his experience during the 1992 Los Angeles riots. In Act I, Coffey describes the first night of rioting. When a crowd hurling rocks descended on the *Times* building, the occupants phoned the police, but received no answer. Coffey reveals that he threatened an intruder who entered through broken windows with the only weapon available—a pair of scissors. Coffey marveled that the crowd seemed to delight in destruction. In Act II, Coffey recounts sadly amusing stories of socialites fearing the fall of Beverly Hills and, more heart wrenching, stories of incredible cruelty. When he looks back, Coffey admires the journalistic efforts of the *Times*. In Act III of his narrative, Coffey examines

Photo on previous page: A banner calling for peace is displayed near a memorial on the grounds of a ruined gas station in a South Central Los Angeles neighborhood in May 1992. (© AP Photo/ Reed Saxon.)

what he calls the Big If, questioning, for example, what might have happened if he had not been at the *Times* when needed. He concludes that, "The inevitable in hindsight is the unimaginable a second before."

T he rocks smashed my office windows just after dark—broken glass all over the carpets of the *Los Angeles Times*'s proud fortress on Spring Street. Down the block, two buildings were on fire. I remember how red the flames looked against the black sky. Chemical fire?, I wondered. Way too close to us, in any case, as were the sirens.

ACT I: First Night

An afternoon of scattered protests around the Southland after the shock of the Rodney King trial verdict had now come right into our house.

What next?

The question in the afternoon had been easier: to deploy or not, before the verdict on the four police officers in the videotaped beating of the speeding black motorist. Newsrooms are not typically great on detailed plans and contingencies. We ran on adrenaline and caffeine and competition, and called ourselves, only a little ironically, "The Masters of Disaster." This time we deployed early, and a damn good thing. Because what came after the astonishing not-guilty verdict that afternoon were three days of intense city-under-siege journalism.

> What came after the astonishing not-guilty verdict that afternoon were three days of intense city-under-siege journalism.

At the end, more than 50 were dead, scores of buildings were burned, looting had become near-epidemic, and the newsroom of the *Times* had been stretched beyond all previous limits. But the end was, as always, not the end.

History is argument without ceasefire. Whose faults showed most blatantly those April days? Was the legal system stacked against blacks, even after that video? Who was a hero, who a fool, who an avenging angel, who a thief (or worse) and why? Questions still up for debate.

What was not up for debate that opening night was that we at the *Times* needed police help. As editor, I called Parker Center (police headquarters), hoping the title might get a little notice on what was looking like a bad night for the fabled LAPD. (Worst ever, it turned out.) The phone rang endlessly, without answer.

Next call was to our own uniformed security guards across the street. In the afternoon, the usual couple-of-hundred protestors had marched at Parker Center, two blocks away. By night, the crowd (multihued, it should be noted) had become a broiling mass. More than a few ripped up pavement from a street project unluckily right beside the *Times* and were hurling away.

"We're pinned in," said our security guard. An unarguable but disheartening reply.

Then I got a call that looters were inside on the street floor. With one of our bravest newsroom administrators, I headed down to defend our . . . what? Our computers? Our sense of order? Our flammable mass of paper?

One intruder was coming through the broken windows. I grabbed a pair of scissors and shouted, "Get out!" Luckily for me, he did.

So I went out and walked through the crowds, looking for why they were attacking us. On my tour, this particular crowd was in carnival spirits—though destruction, not sex, was the delight of the evening. It's catching, as crowd psychologists will tell you.

I called to check on my wife, an emergency-room doctor, on duty that night in comparatively quiet Pasadena. Don't go out there anymore, she told me—your Brooks Brothers suit won't fit in. She said that she saw, as patients, a lot of the people who likely were in the streets, and I would be better off editing the copy and letting the newsroom's Masters of Disaster report from the field.

They did. In fact they later won, for magnificent work sometimes literally under the gun, a richly deserved Pulitzer Prize. But that was a long way away—as was the day, five years later, when I left the *Times* and was given the pair of scissors that had achieved high status in the retelling.

Today the scissors sit, among my souvenirs, with a window-smashing boulder from the street. My very own Rock, Paper, Scissors from the night Los Angeles exploded.

ACT II: 'Has Beverly Hills Fallen Yet?'

What's most chilling in life arrives when the normal turns lethal. Sweet birds, in an Alfred Hitchcock movie, become killers, a cold becomes pneumonia, the hitchhiker so companionably chatting for 30 minutes turns to face you with a murderer's smile along a lonely stretch of road. . . .

In Los Angeles, what brought hairs rising on the back of your neck was that the rioting did not stop in the cold light of the day after. Or the next night. Or the next day. The police were overwhelmed, in disarray. The National Guard was delayed (could it be?) because they had too little ammunition.

> What stands out most . . . are the individual voices—often from hearts torn by their city in flames and by the cruelty, often racial, revealed and remembered.

What stands out most, reading the coverage 20 years later, are the individual voices—often from hearts torn by their city in flames and by the cruelty, often racial, revealed and remembered.

One aging Angeleno socialite asked a reporter, "Has Beverly Hills fallen yet?" Comic in a way, but who knows what falling cities she may have fled in earlier days. Her question became a mocking slogan for several in the newsroom, always eager for new surprises. That, and "The Riot Diet" some went on: Ice cream by the pint, late at night. . . . Five sleepy hours later, Dunkin Donuts and coffee by the quart. . . . Then back to the coverage.

Rumors were bloody, but reality could be worse. Helicopters hovered over unlucky white trucker Reginald Denny being beaten into the street, with a rock thrown thunderously onto his head. His black assailants did a victory dance.

Photos of Korean merchants, armed and defiant, defending their stores from the torch added to the nightmare mosaic of multiethnic LA.

What had the understandable anguish over the not-guilty verdict turned into? The biggest decision of our coverage was to try to answer that in a series of five special sections, each day the week after the riots.

Our publisher David Laventhol gave us the expensive white space and fine ideas. Even as we continued to cover endless calls for calm from leaders of very many stripes (Rodney King himself: "Can we all get along?" No.), we planned "Understanding the Riots"—building the plane as we flew it.

Looking at the sections today, the Shakespearean range of motives and destinies is still striking.

"The Path to Fury" was the first, recalling the Watts riots of 1965. Antagonism between the police and the black communities echoed down the decades (and would again soon, and famously, with the O.J. Simpson trial).

We took a Studs Terkel approach in another section—short interviews of Angelenos from all walks about the impact of the riots. Studs himself grinned and grabbed reflected glory when he visited later.

"Seeing Ourselves" was a collection of datelines from our then-large foreign and national staffs about how Los Angeles looked from afar—from other capitals, like then-apartheid Johannesburg and then-booming Tokyo (that one titled "Sympathy, Tinged with Contempt.")

In Afghanistan, our correspondent reported that the unrest in Los Angeles was used at press conferences by contending warlords to show that recent killings in Kabul were, comparatively, not so bad.

I wonder how many of those warlords are still alive? Our correspondent is not. The brilliant Mark Fineman, a newsroom combination of Errol Flynn and Humphrey Bogart, dead in Baghdad, heart attack, 2003, age 51. His name is on the smoked glass wall of the Journalists Memorial at the Newseum in Washington D.C. where I work today, and it never fails to bring the sharp pang of nostalgia and loss and admiration—which is my enduring feeling for the men and women of the Los Angeles Times and their coverage of the Days of Rage in 1992.

ACT III: Aftermath—The Big If

A letter concerning our coverage came a few days later from a longtime journalistic hero, Gay Talese, author of *The Kingdom and the Power,* an epic about *The New York Times*. "I guess that great newspapers are at their greatest when the challenge demands it," he wrote, "and thus the *Los Angeles Times* these last several days has set rare standards in reporting—to which I (along with many thousands of others) would like to offer my congratulations.

"I myself was particularly impressed by the two personal accounts on yesterday's front page by Elaine Woo and Part Morrison. Here their personal voices and backgrounds lent a dimension to the on-going developments that was unique and so appropriate: and it was admirable too, that the editors put these well-written essays on the front page."

Indeed, what stands out most, reading the coverage 20 years later, are the individual voices—often from hearts torn by their city in flames and by the cruelty, often racial, revealed and remembered.

No surprise, Gay Talese did not have the last word on our coverage. We were attacked on the op-ed pages of the *Wall Street Journal* for not sufficiently condemning the rioters in enough places—an acid, highly selective piece that prefigured the polarized debates of today. Luckily, the author missed a couple of key points, so I struck back in a Letter to the Editor the next day and landed hard left hooks.

During the riots, one of our able editors had said in a meeting that we were using black journalists as "cannon fodder." She had not realized the comment would go public (we've all been there). But that jibe made the press when least needed. So we later painstakingly went back and recounted, by ethnicity, each assignment, to each area, during the riots.

We found we had done pretty well fielding a balanced team in areas of higher and lower risk. The Catch-22 here was that an enduring blemish of the *Times*'s coverage of the Watts riots of 1965 had been the dearth of black reporters; a black advertising staffer helped fill the breach and reported from Watts, where he did an admirable job. After the report on the reporters was made public, the complaint became that we had mostly white editors making the key decisions.

> [What] if only a print reporter, not a video camera, had recorded the King beating [or] if the video had been edited to show King's earlier provocative actions . . . ?

Another one of the Big Ifs of the L.A. riots (the term comes from the risk-analysis profession to provoke counterfactual analysis: "If Hitler had won the Battle of Britain, then . . . ?"): If only a print reporter, not a video camera, had recorded the King beating, then . . . ? If the video had been edited to show King's earlier provocative actions, then . . . ?

If the jury had explained their reasoning in a public and forthright manner, then . . . ?

If Rodney King's Hyundai, clocked at 100 mph (?!?), had outrun the police, then . . . ?

The lesson of counterfactuals is that destiny often teeters on a narrow ledge. The inevitable in hindsight is the unimaginable a second before.

I have my own Big If from the first night. My teenage son and I were scheduled to go the Greek Theatre to see singer Lou Reed ("Walk on the Wild Side"). As the demonstrations got uglier, I decided not to go. He called to appeal—yet another disappointment from journalist dad—I wavered, then firmed.

I might have wound up like LAPD Chief Daryl Gates that night—out of position on the West Side, when most needed.

My son wound up barely making it home from the Greek through the burning city to his highly anxious mother. At 2 A.M. the last edition of the paper was "put to bed," so I set off through Chinatown ("Forget it, Jake"), to my home near the Rose Bowl.

I was driving a Corvette in those California days, a gift from my wife, with a booming sound system. I put on N.W.A.'s "Straight Outta Compton" to keep me awake. I pulled into the driveway with the "F--- tha Police" anthem roaring. (Even now, with several police officers as personal friends, I feel compelled to add I was listening as a sleep-deprived journalist, not as an advocate.)

> What would you have thought the night of the riots if a car pulled in your driveway at 2:30 A.M., booming Ice Cube, Dr. Dre, and Eazy-E?

As I opened the door to my house, a scene from *Nightmare on Elm Street* started to explode. A baseball bat was rising toward my head.

My son, the strong protector of his home and sleeping mother, stopped just in time.

What would you have thought the night of the riots if a car pulled in your driveway at 2:30 A.M., booming Ice

Cube, Dr. Dre, and Eazy-E? Still, if the bat had sent me to the next world, then this journalistic immortality of a sort might have been mine:

Headline: "Los Angeles Times Editor Killed on Own Front Porch During Riots—Loud Gangsta Rap Music Blamed."

Years later, I might have become a *Jeopardy* question — likely in one of the lower-priced categories.

Big If.

A National Guardsman Shares His Experience Patrolling Riot-Torn South Los Angeles

Chuck DeVore

At the time of the 1992 Los Angeles riots, Chuck DeVore was a captain in the National Guard. In the following viewpoint, he relates his experience when called to duty in Los Angeles. His unit received a few hours of training designed for mass demonstrations, not urban warfare. Nevertheless, early on the morning of May 1, 1992, his convoy secured a parking structure that would become their command center, and his unit began to patrol. People in the neighborhood had mixed reactions to their arrival. While the middle-class residents cheered, gang members threatened them as they passed. However, when gang members learned that the National Guard could shoot to kill, they became less aggressive. Captain DeVore worked with his team to ensure that they did not overreact, even when flyers posted in the neighborhood urged violence. In the end, DeVore learned two lessons: civilization is fragile and when it breaks down, people should be prepared to defend themselves.

L ike charred fingers clawing skyward, columns of thick black smoke rose from a burning Los Angeles. It was April 30, 1992, and I was flying into Long Beach from the San Francisco Bay area to join my Army National Guard unit to patrol the riot-battered city.

Life Was Good

Twenty-four hours before, I was working on a classified missile defense program for Lockheed. My wife and infant daughter had traveled with me and were staying at a nearby Residence Inn. Life was good. Only a year before, I was unemployed—laid-off during a few months of active duty in support of the Gulf War.

I went back to the hotel on the evening of April 29 to the news of the near-beating death of trucker Reginald Denny in the aftermath the acquittal of the four Los Angeles Police Department officers charged with using excessive force during their arrest of Rodney King after a drunken King led them on a high speed chase and then resisted once the police pulled him over. At 9 P.M., Governor Pete Wilson called out 2,000 National Guard troops, but my unit, a tank battalion headquartered in National City just south of San Diego, wasn't among them.

By early morning on the 30th, the violence appeared to have died down. I went to work.

The great InterWeb/Twitter/Facebook complex was as yet unformed. The World Wide Web wouldn't get its first graphical browser until the following year. Working in the classified security vault, I was clueless about the events that started to spiral out of control 400 miles to south in Los Angeles by mid-morning.

A Call to Duty

By lunchtime, L.A.'s mayor, Tom Bradley, declared a dusk-to-dawn curfew. A television set was switched on in the program bay where I was working. A colleague walked by and said, "Aren't you in the National Guard?" then gestured at the TV where images of burning buildings and looters filled the screen.

I called my wife and told her to be prepared to fly by the afternoon. She checked our answering machine at home, but the National Guard hadn't yet left a phone tree message calling me up to active duty (in 1992, few people had cell phones which were very expensive and as large as walkie-talkies). I called my unit and they said it was very likely we would be activated.

We flew back home that afternoon, Los Angeles burning below us as the sun set over the Pacific.

I grabbed my gear at home and linked up with my National Guard unit at an armory in Long Beach.

We trained for a few hours in the parking lot amidst camouflaged trucks—although the training seemed wholly irrelevant to the mission at hand, since it was geared towards handling a circa 1960s mass demonstration rather than the urban warfare-like environment [we] were about to enter.

Since the Guard had been told by law enforcement not to worry about a civil disturbance associated with the trial verdict, the Guard had loaned some of its riot control equipment to law enforcement. Finally, face shields and flak vests showed up, then the ammunition. The delay in the ammunition was a classic instance of unintended consequences: in a move designed to save money, bureaucratic paperwork, and reduce the threat of terrorists or criminals stealing ammunition and weapons from an armory, all ammunition had been centralized at a base in the middle of the state, some 220 miles away. Without ammo, the Guardsman would have been vulnerable and of questionable effectiveness, given the intensity of the violence. Lastly, as an officer (I was a captain then), I was issued two military-grade tear gas (CS) grenades.

Setting Up a Parking Lot Command Center

Early in the morning on May 1, we formed into a convoy and made our way to the area that would be our home for the next few days: the Baldwin Hills Crenshaw Plaza at the corner of Crenshaw and Martin Luther King, Jr. Boulevard.

> As I was puzzling over why anyone would bother to burn down a drive-through, a burning car came into view, then another.

A burning fast food joint greeted us as we pulled onto Crenshaw, a couple of miles from our destination. As I was puzzling over why anyone would bother to burn down a drive-through, a burning car came into view, then another. A small group of looters in a strip mall, intent on increasing their material worth, ignored us as we rumbled by.

As we pulled into the large shopping mall, our advance party was dispersing and arresting a group of about 50 looters. We secured the parking structure. Our command group made its way to the L.A.P.D.'s South L.A. homicide and traffic division office in back of the ground level of the parking garage. The officers there were visibly relieved, saying that an angry mob had formed outside their steel doors just before we arrived.

The police gave us a quick overview of the neighborhood, drawing our attention to the neighborhood to the southwest, off of Santa Rosalia Drive, calling it "The Jungle" for its frequent violence caused, they said, by racial strife between the Mexican-Americans and African-Americans who lived there.

Our armor battalion of about 350 tankers began to send out patrols, sans armor, both mounted and on foot.

Cars were burning everywhere. Looters had stolen cars to use as battering rams to break into liquor stores and electronics shops. People even shot at firefighters who responded to the many fires. Armed escort was needed for the fire trucks.

We learned that armed men on rooftops were the good guys, mostly Korean shop owners protecting their life's investment. The armed men on the street were the hostiles.

Of the 53 people who were killed during the 1992 L.A. Riots—19 more than died in the 1965 Watts Riots—two were Asian, and one of those deaths was due to a "friendly fire" incident in which two groups of Korean shop owners mistook the other for looters. Despite their shops and liquor stores being frequently singled out for arson and looting, the Korean immigrants made full use of their uniquely American Second Amendment rights, protecting themselves and their property during a multi-day breakdown in law and order.

Diverse Reactions

As we went out on patrol that day, the residents of the largely middle class African-American neighborhood to the east of the mall called out, "God Bless the National Guard!"

Gang members, up by Noon after a long night of looting, had a different reaction. They threatened our troops, flashing gang signs, thick gold chains hanging off their necks.

Late that afternoon, a stray bullet shattered the back passenger window of a car parked about 30 feet from where I was operating in our battalion HQ.

We found out that President George H.W. Bush was federalizing us, bringing the California National Guard under U.S. government control. The President addressed the nation, saying that he would "use whatever force is necessary" to quell the "random terror and lawlessness."

Unbeknownst to the California National Guard troops on the scene, Secretary of Defense [Dick] Cheney had put 4,000 active duty soldiers and Marines on alert the day before.

As night began to fall, I led my first of three foot patrols. I formed up the squad of eight and took point, asking a Vietnam veteran staff sergeant to follow. He had grown up in the neighborhood and, being African-American, I thought he might reduce the tension should we encounter difficulty. As soon as we stepped onto Crenshaw, the sergeant locked and loaded. Instantly, I heard the other troops do the same. I stopped and turned around. "Take the rounds out of your chambers," I said, "This is America, not Lebanon, if someone takes me out, you'll have plenty of time to lock and load." Our orders were to patrol with loaded magazines, but no round in the chamber.

Around midnight, we heard a commotion in "The Jungle." We jogged over to investigate. It was nothing more than a domestic dispute between a very drunken man and his very irate woman. She kept saying she was going to kill him. I told them that they needed to get off the street—that there was a curfew. She reluctantly headed for home, escorted by a soldier. I asked the man to decamp for home, "But she'll kill me!" he slurred. I thought, that might be so, but she'll have to do it in the house, not on the street. We took him home too, after he dumped the rest of his whiskey down the storm drain, a dozen sets of eyes looking down on our squad from the unlit windows of the adjacent two-story apartment.

The next patrol almost turned tragically comic. A shiny all-black sedan slowly rolled towards us, head lights off. It was tricked out with chrome rims and looked like a drug baron's ride. The windows were part-way down. I deployed the squad into an "L" at the intersection, signaling them to be prepared for what we thought was an attempted drive-by gang shooting. I shouted out, "Halt! There's a curfew. What's your business?" The car lurched to a halt. I could see frenzied activity in the unlit car. Then a high-pitched, somewhat cracking voice, said from the driver's side, "L.A.P.D. vice squad!" A hand extended police ID. I was incredulous. The vice squad was patrolling at night in a darkened, unmarked car as buildings still burned and thousands of nervous Guardsmen patrolled the streets they were unable to control.

Confusion over the Guard's Authority

By May 2, I had been awake for more than 36 hours straight, patrolling on foot and on the back of trucks and HUMVEEs.

> The [LAPD] vice squad was patrolling at night in a darkened, unmarked cars as buildings still burned and thousands of nervous Guardsmen patrolled the streets [the LAPD] were unable to control.

It was then that we learned that federal troops were arriving and would take over command of the operation. Our morale plummeted—especially as we had quelled the violence within 24 hours of our arrival in the city and saw little need for the active duty to "save the day." Further, with more advance notice, the 1,500 U.S. Marines and 2,000 U.S. Army soldiers took longer to muster into L.A. than did 10,000 Guard members, a force of citizen-soldiers launching into action with no advance warning. Hours later, the 7th Infantry Division commander assumed command of the joint U.S. Army-US. Marine Corps force, placing the National Guard commanding general in charge of all Army forces, both Guard and Active Duty, our honor restored, morale bounced back.

Since National Guard members usually operate under control of their respective governors in peacetime, the Posse Comitatus Act restrictions against federal troops assisting in civilian law enforcement duties doesn't apply to them. That changed on May 2, however, when the military lawyers from the 7th Infantry Division mistakenly thought that the Guard's federalization compelled us to act within the confines of Posse Comitatus. Immediately, our close cooperation with the L.A.P.D. was scaled back by the active duty general.

In fact, when President Bush signed Executive Order 12804 on May 1, invoking the Insurrection Act, he authorized the Army and Marines, as well as the federalized National Guard, to enforce civilian law to help restore law and order. Had Wikipedia been available in 1992, the 7th Infantry Division JAG officers (military lawyers) might have come to a different conclusion.

Flyers urging violence against law enforcement in service of the "insurrection" were commonplace during the riots. The flyers were written and printed by Communist organizations—which seemed ironic, given the fall of the Berlin Wall only two-and-a-half years before. Strangely enough, the El Salvadoran Communist guerilla group FMLN (Farabundo Martí National Liberation Front) has an ongoing presence in Los Angeles, where they participate in the city's annual May Day parade, carrying their red banners.

Quelling Defiance

On May 3, with the military taking a lower profile, gang members began to show more defiance. Rumors were flying around that the military had no ammunition or wasn't allowed to shoot. We were very concerned about what might happen the next night when Mayor Tom Bradley was expected to lift the nighttime curfew.

As fate would have it, a gang member wannabe tried to run over a team of Guardsmen at a checkpoint. On his third pass to try to kill the soldiers, they fired 10 rounds at the tires of the onrushing car. He pressed on towards the checkpoint. So, the soldiers shifted fire, killing him with two bullets to the head and one in the shoulder.

The next morning, the gang members wouldn't even look us in the eye as we made a limited number of patrols. They knew the Guard could shoot to kill.

During the far less destructive Watts Riots in 1965, a considerable amount of ammunition was expended, up to and including .50 caliber heavy machine gun rounds. In the 1992 riots, the National Guard only fired 20 rounds—a remarkable affirmation of restraint and training.

> In the 1992 riots, the National Guard only fired 20 rounds—a remarkable affirmation of restraint and training.

People opined that the riots in 1992 were entirely predictable, when looking at the area's recession-time high unemployment and poverty rate of between 20 and 40 percent. Today, South Los Angeles (formerly known as South-Central Los Angeles) has a poverty rate of 30 percent, about the same as in 1992. The area's demographics have shifted significantly, however, moving from Hispanics, mainly Mexican-Americans and African Americans comprising 47 percent each in 1990 to today, wherein Latinos outnumber blacks two to one.

There are two valuable lessons from the 1992 Los Angeles riots. First, civilization has a very, very thin veneer that can break down suddenly and with little warning (there were sympathy riots up and down the West Coast and unrest in other urban areas). Second, when civilization does break down, law enforcement is virtually powerless for a time during which a judicious exercise of one's Second Amendment rights may be all that stands between you and destructive anarchy.

A Minister Tours the Aftermath of the Los Angeles Riots

Jim Conn

Reverend Jim Conn was a student at the University of California, in Santa Barbara, during the Watts riots in 1965. He wanted to see for himself the aftermath of the Los Angeles riots in 1992. The day after the riots erupted, Conn got in his car and toured the streets of South Los Angeles. He shares his observations in the following viewpoint. He notes people pushing shopping carts filled with stolen goods and police cars with nervous officers. Although dismayed that many churches were closed, he talked to one minister who had stayed behind to calm rampaging kids and visited another with whom he watched the burning city in sadness. Conn reflects that following the 1992 riots, people began to look at the community's assets rather than its weaknesses, a change he believes offers hope. Conn served on the Santa Monica City Council and as the city's mayor; he also helped found Clergy and Laity United for Economic Justice, Los Angeles.

SOURCE. Jim Conn, "1992 Remembered: Driving into the Wreck," *The Frying Pan*, April 19, 2012. www.fryingpannews.org. Copyright © 2012 by Los Angeles Alliance for a New Economy. All rights reserved. Reproduced by permission.

It was a Wednesday night and my son was watching the news on TV in his room while I fixed dinner. "Dad," he called from the bedroom, "Dad, you better get in here and see this."

"This" turned out to be the beginnings of the worst urban social upheaval in American history. Its early moments were caught on film by a news helicopter high over the intersection of Florence and Normandie. We watched, transfixed, as some black kids pulled a white truck driver out of his cab and one of them hit him with a brick. An Asian woman was threatened as she tried to make a right turn off Normandie onto Florence, her face etched with fear. Car windows were broken. The news commentators called them "hoodlums" and the police were nowhere in sight. Then we watched as the city began to burn.

> I wanted to see for myself what the aftermath of a night of riots looked like.

Viewing the Aftermath

I was an undergrad at UC Santa Barbara when Watts upended L.A. in 1965, and now, in 1992, I wanted to see for myself what the aftermath of a night of riots looked like. So I put on my clerical collar—my defense against universal disorder—climbed in my old VW bug, and drove the streets of South L.A. I haphazardly drove to every United Methodist Church south of the I-10. From Vernon and Budlong to Normandie and 65th Street, to Grammercy near Manchester, over to 85th and Main, down past 103rd and Central, then back north toward the I-10.

The streets were relatively quiet in the morning-after hangover. Not many cars. Police units with officers crammed in, four-to-a-car, guns bristling. Latino families pushing shopping carts from looted supermarkets piled high with boxes of diapers, bottled water, canned food.

Every church I saw—including the ones I passed that weren't Methodist, were locked up, closed. The ministers were home safe, apparently. Except for an older minister I knew at one place. He had spent the night at the church, he told me. He knew the gangs in the neighborhood and in the early morning hours he had pushed a flaming mattress away from a wall of the community center across the street that the church operated. Alone, he had talked down some kids in the neighborhood who were on a rampage.

Later up on West Adams, my long-time mentor, Rev. Jim Lawson, was also at his church, Holman United Methodist. He was the one who had invited Martin Luther King Jr. to Memphis to support the garbage workers' strike and who had trained Nashville's non-violent demonstrators. From his office window we now watched the smoke curling up from a dozen fires around the basin. We felt saddened by the events and the destruction, and we were aware of how much more there was to come before things turned around.

Examining Two Different Responses

In 1965, the official response examined the *needs* in South L.A.: the bureaucracy of welfare, the neglect of schools, the absence of supermarkets, the segregated housing, the dearth of hospitals, the barest representation at City Hall, an occupying force of a nearly all-white police force. These were the results of a white Los Angeles that was not paying attention. As my then-bishop at the time said, "I didn't know."

In 1992 the response looked at the *assets* of South Los Angeles. Bankers took bus tours to places they had never seen and realized there were healthy loan opportunities there. Studies examined the amount of groceries people from the area purchased but could not buy in South Los Angeles, so firms promised to build supermarkets and strip malls. The school district geared up the largest municipal bond issue in American history to build new schools across the inner city. The media acknowledged and acclaimed the richness and diversity of cultural experience throughout the area. The city identified 52,000 jobs in South L.A.—where conventional wisdom said there were none—and initiated job creation and work-readiness projects.

In 1965 Los Angeles looked at the neglected *needs* of South Los Angeles. In 1992 it focused on *asset* analysis and the results attracted investments from both private and public sectors. The work is not done. Some of it has stalled, but in the aftermath of that upheaval the tone and the tenor shifted—and even the results—from despair to possibility. Those were changes my son and I would never have imagined as we sat in his room that night watching TV as L.A. burned.

A Korean-American Journalist Tours Koreatown During the Riots

Dexter H. Kim

In the following viewpoint, Korean-American journalist Dexter H. Kim tells his 1992 Los Angeles riots story. On the second day of rioting, he walked the streets of Koreatown while its stores were looted and burned. Rioters targeted Korean-owned businesses, and Kim talked to some of the merchants who armed themselves and took to the rooftops to protect their stores. On Saturday, Kim attended a rally that hoped to promote peace and reconciliation. Many Korean-Americans carried US flags and shouted that they loved the black community, but anger was also evident—anger at the police, the media, and the people they worked so hard to serve. Indeed, Kim could feel the rage in those who came to the United States to build a better life only to have their hopes destroyed. At the rally, however, he felt great pride when he heard people chant, "We love L.A."

As I stand at the edge of Koreatown Thursday afternoon [April 30, 1992] watching the wave of looters wash up Vermont Avenue, I'm reminded of the climactic fistfight at the end of *Blazing Saddles*. The approaching mayhem and pandemonium seems like a riot scene broken out of some studio back lot and spilling out onto the streets of Los Angeles.

Walking Through Koreatown

Perhaps the thought of Mel Brooks and the scene's utter surrealism keeps me from panicking and getting the hell out of there. Or maybe it's plain stupidity. I am, after all, a Korean-American in a place and time where even looking Korean can get you beaten or killed. As I make my way through Koreatown while one Korean store after another is being gutted, looted and set aflame, even the riot's festival atmosphere doesn't keep me from pulling my ball cap lower over my eyes.

> I make my way through Koreatown while one Korean store after another is being gutted, looted and set aflame.

Even before the acquittal of the four LAPD officers involved in the Rodney King beating, even before Soon Ja Du's probation sentence in the Latasha Harlins killing, Korean-Americans in L.A. have fretted over being victimized by crime. Statistics only confirm their fears. In Koreatown during 1991, the LAPD reported 48 murders, 84 rapes, 1,837 thefts, 2,024 burglaries, 2,102 assaults, 2,527 robberies, and 6,270 auto thefts and burglaries. With more than 1,867 Korean-owned businesses vandalized, looted or burned citywide (according to Radio Korea), the riot was the fulfillment of the Korean-American merchants' worst nightmares.

"Is that an *Uzi* that guy is carrying?" Paul Moyer asks during one of television's less analytic moments of the riot coverage.

Defending Livelihoods

Determined to defend their livelihoods, many frightened and/or courageous Korean-American vigilantes take up arms to repel the coming onslaught of marauders. At California Market on Western Avenue, employees armed with pistols and shotguns barricade the windows and entrances with shopping carts, bags of rice and wooden platforms. At the riot's height, many Korean-Americans rush to defend markets at the urgent request of shop owners broadcasting over Korean-language radio stations KCB 93.5 FM and Radio Korea 1580 AM.

> Determined to defend their livelihoods, many frightened and/or courageous Korean-American vigilantes take up arms to repel the coming onslaught of marauders.

The broadcasts saved many stores, but at least one death resulted from the calls for volunteers. Eighteen-year-old Edward Song Lee, responding to a radio plea for help, was shot and killed during a confusing crossfire in which volunteers and Korean security guards apparently mistook one another for looters.

On Friday afternoon, I head for the Olympic Discount Swap Meet in east Koreatown where Channel 7 had spotted the Uzi-toting security guard. Clambering to the rooftop, I find some young Korean-American men who had spent the night guarding the building against attack. Except for a few sticks and baseball bats, the weapons are gone. I ask about the guns. They've been stored in the trunks of cars surrounding the swap meet, out of sight but within reach should they be needed. Both

tense and tired from the night before, the young men are reluctant to talk.

"Why did you come to defend this store and not somewhere else?" I ask one of them.

"Because," he says as if the answer were self-evident, "we heard this place was the most dangerous."

A Plea for Peace

On my way to Saturday morning's rally at Ardmore Recreation Center on San Marino, I stop my car for a Korean woman who asks if I could give her elderly mother and grandmother a ride to the park.

"*Ne, ne,*" I say. "Climb in."

Wearing a traditional *hanbok* dress and carrying a small American flag, the grandmother turns to me, "*Hankook mal halju asayo?*"

A gathering in Los Angeles's Koreatown on May 1, 1992, promotes peace in reaction to the widespread violence of the preceding two days. (© **Dayna Smith/ The Washington Post/ Getty Images.**)

"Aniyo, halmoni," I reply. "I'm 2.5 generation. My Korean is very bad."

Obviously not understanding my English, she smiles and leans back in her scat, clutching her flag.

By the time I reach the park, about 30,000 people, mostly Korean-American, have gathered. They're here to listen to speeches given by community leaders, and to begin the process of cleaning up and, later, to march the length of Koreatown in a plea for peace.

Some lack the English to even attempt the "We want justice! We want peace!" cry, but it doesn't stop them from shouting a close approximation. Others struggle with English on their signs and banners. "WE LOVE BLACK," reads one. One woman's name tag declares, "Hello, my name is KOREAN."

Beneath Saturday's plea for peace and reconciliation, however, are the Korean-American community's underlying feelings of anger, abandonment and betrayal—betrayal by the LAPD, by politicians, by the media and by the communities they work so hard to service.

Leaving South Central

Many merchants find it hard to understand why their stores have been looted and burned. Some of them believe Korean stores were hard hit because of the type of businesses Koreans tend to own: liquor and grocery stores. Others argue that because of the large number of shops owned by Koreans in South-Central L.A. and Koreatown, the destruction of a large number of Korean stores is only a matter of percentages. Other store owners, however, feel they were targeted by a vindictive crowd.

"We were serving them," says one merchant at the rally. "Where are they going to go now?"

Although Korean-Americans have made it clear they want to rebuild Koreatown, they are far less likely to return to South-Central. While many Korean-American merchants have continued to do business in those areas, an increasing number reside in the quieter suburbs of L.A. and Orange County.

"Why should they go back there?" one Korean-American man asks me during the march. "There's plenty of other places they can go."

Over the past week, I have spoken with people who came to the United States with the hope of building a better life for themselves and their children, and watched those hopes reduced to rubble in a few days of rage. Walking down the same street on Saturday where just two days earlier I had seen those hopes in flames, my heart swells to twice its normal size while tens of thousands of those people chant, "We love L.A."

1991

March 2   After drinking heavily while watching a basketball game, Rodney King drives friends Bryan Adams and Freddie Helms on Interstate 210 in Los Angeles.

March 3   At approximately 12:30 AM, California Highway Patrol officers Tim and Melanie Singer attempt to initiate a traffic stop. A high-speed pursuit ensues at speeds up to 115 mph over Los Angeles freeways and residential streets. After cutting off King's vehicle, the Singers attempt to arrest King with guns drawn.

Four Los Angeles Police Department (LAPD) officers—Sergeant Stacey Koon, Laurence Powell, Timothy Wind, and Theodore Briseno—intervene.

George Holliday shoots an amateur video from the balcony of his apartment that shows three police officers striking King over fifty times with metal batons while a fourth officer watches before handcuffing him. King is taken to a hospital by ambulance.

March 4   Holliday releases his videotape to the Los Angeles television station KTLA. The station takes the tape to LAPD headquarters where it is viewed by senior officers. KTLA later that night broadcasts the videotape on the evening news.

March 5   CNN obtains a copy of the Holliday videotape and plays it on its nationwide cable news program. The FBI opens an investigation of the King beating.

March 6   All major networks broadcast the Holliday videotape on evening news programs. King is released from jail without charges.

March 7   Los Angeles Police Chief Daryl Gates announces that the officers involved in the King beating will be prosecuted.

March 8   District Attorney Ira Reiner announces that he will seek indictments against the four officers.

March 10   A *Los Angeles Times* poll reports that 92 percent of those who had seen the Holliday videotape thought excessive force had been used against King.

March 14   After watching the videotape and listening to testimony, a grand jury returns indictments against all four officers.

April 1   Los Angeles mayor Tom Bradley announces that a commission headed by Warren Christopher will evaluate LAPD performance.

April 2   Mayor Bradley asks for the resignation of Police Chief Gates; Gates refuses.

May 16   Judge Bernard Kamins sets June 17 as the opening date for the trial and denies a change of venue to a location outside of Los Angeles. The defense appeals.

June 23   The California Court of Appeals grants the change of venue and reassigns the case to Judge Stanley Weisberg when Judge Kamins sends a message to prosecutors, claiming, "Don't panic. You can trust me."

November 26   Judge Weisberg transfers the case to the predominantly white, conservative Simi Valley.

1992

February 3   The trial begins.

March 2   A jury of ten whites, one Hispanic, and one Filipino-American is finally selected. Six are male and six female.

April 29   3:15 PM: The Simi Valley jury acquits all four officers charged in the beating.

5: 25 PM: Police respond to the intersection of Florence and Normandie as people throw beer cans at passing motorists. The police retreat and do not return for nearly three hours.

6:30 PM: Angry demonstrators gather outside the Parker Center, Los Angeles police headquarters. Police Chief Daryl Gates declares his officers are dealing with the situation "calmly, maturely, professionally." He leaves to attend a Brentwood fundraiser to campaign against Charter Amendment F, a police reform ballot measure.

6:45 PM: Journalists Bob Tur and Marika Gerrard broadcast live pictures from a helicopter of truck driver Reginald Denny being dragged from the cab of his truck and beaten nearly to death at the intersection of Florence and Normandie Avenues.

8:30 PM: Gates returns to the city's Emergency Response Center.

8:45 PM: Mayor Tom Bradley calls a local state of emergency. Moments later, Governor Pete Wilson orders the National Guard to activate two thousand reserve soldiers.

9:04 PM: The California Highway Patrol closes exit ramps off the Harbor Freeway from the Santa Monica Freeway junction to Century Boulevard to keep motorists from wandering into the path of violence.

11:00 PM: Mayor Bradley in a televised address says the city will "take whatever resources needed" to quell the violence. He asks people to stay off the streets.

April 30   12:15 AM: Mayor Bradley declares a dusk-to-dawn curfew in the city and county of Los Angeles. He also prohibits the sale of ammunition and gasoline, other than for use in cars.

6:00 AM: The riots disrupt life from South Los Angeles to Pasadena. People are asked to stay home from work, bus service is canceled, mail delivery is halted, professional baseball and basketball games are canceled, and schools are closed.

8:00 AM: The National Guard arrives but is not deployed until later as the ammunition for their weapons has not yet arrived, and the police are unsure how they should be used.

12:00 PM: The National Guard is deployed and troops take up position in city hot spots.

11:59 PM: Mayor Bradley and Governor Wilson announce they have requested more Guard troops and ask for US military help.

May 1   1:00 PM: Koreatown merchants arm themselves to protect against looters and firebombs, and more than one thousand Korean Americans gather at a peace rally at Western Avenue and Wilshire Boulevard.

2:45 PM: Rodney King makes an emotional plea for calm, asking, "People, I just want to say, can we all get along? Can we get along? Can we stop making it horrible for the older people and the kids?"

3:00 PM: Approximately four thousand federal troops arrive at Marine Corps Air Stations in Tustin and El Toro, California.

9:03 PM: President George H.W. Bush speaks to the American people from the Oval Office of the White House, assuring that order will be restored and justice served, while condemning LA rioters.

May 2   8:00 AM: The first of six thousand alleged looters and arsonists are scheduled to appear in court, but due to the large volume, arraignments are delayed until the afternoon.

11:00 AM: Approximately thirty thousand people march in support of racial healing and for the merchants of Koreatown.

4:00 PM: US Marine units arrive in Compton, a city southwest of Los Angeles notorious for its heavy concentration of gangs and gang violence.

May 3   10:30 AM: Reverend Jesse Jackson meets with Koreatown leaders to urge an end to animosity between African American and Korean American communities.

11:30 AM: Mayor Bradley announces that the curfew will be lifted on Monday, May 4 and expects inquiries into LAPD and National Guard delays in responding to the crisis.

1:00 PM: Harbor Freeway off-ramps reopen.

May 4   Although street corners are guarded by rifle-toting soldiers, Los Angeles residents return to work.

May 11   Former FBI Director William H. Webster directs an investigation of the LAPD's heavily criticized response to the riots.

August 4   A federal grand jury returns indictments against the four acquitted officers on charges of violating the civil rights of Rodney King.

October 21   The Webster Commission concludes that the LAPD and City Hall failed to plan for civil disorder prior to the verdict.

December 7   Damien Monroe "Football" Williams is convicted of throwing a brick at the head of truck driver Denny during the riots and is sentenced to ten years in prison.

1993

April 16   A federal jury convicts Koon and Powell on one charge of violating King's civil rights. Wind and Briseno are found not guilty. No disturbances follow the verdict.

August 4   US District Judge John Davies sentences both Koon and Powell to thirty months in prison for violating King's civil rights.

1994

April 19   The US District Court in Los Angeles awards King $3.8 million in compensatory damages in a civil lawsuit against the city of Los Angeles. His suit demanded

$56 million—$1 million for every blow struck by LAPD officers.

1995   Powell, then Koon, are released on December 13–14.

2002/2012   Analysts and commentators nationwide revisit the Los Angeles riots on the tenth and twentieth anniversary of the violence.

2012   Rodney King is found dead in his swimming pool on June 17.

FOR FURTHER READING

Books

Kamran Afary, *Performance and Activism: Grassroots Discourses After the Los Angeles Rebellion of 1992*. Lanham, MD: Lexington Books, 2009.

Gregory Alan-Williams, *A Gathering of Heroes: Reflections on Rage and Responsibility: A Memoir of the Los Angeles Riots*. Chicago: Academy Chicago Publishers, 1994.

Amnesty International, *United States of America: Torture, Ill-Treatment and Excessive Force by Police in Los Angeles, California*. New York: Amnesty International Publications, 1992.

Mark Baldassare, ed., *The Los Angeles Riots: Lessons for the Urban Future*. Boulder, CO: Westview, 1994.

Lou Cannon, *Official Negligence: How Rodney King and Riots Changed Los Angeles and the LAPD*. New York: Basic Books, 1999.

James D. Delk, *Fires and Furies: The Los Angeles Riots of 1992*. Palm Springs, CA: ETC Publications, 1995.

Kathi Georges and Jennifer Joseph, eds., *The Verdict Is In*. San Francisco, CA: Manic D Press, 1992.

Robert Gooding-Williams, ed., *Reading Rodney King/Reading Urban Uprising*. New York: Routledge, 1991.

Sue L. Hamilton, *Los Angeles Riots*. Edina, MN: Abdo & Daughters, 1992.

Don Hazen, ed., *Inside the L.A. Riots: What Really Happened—and Why It Will Happen Again*. New York: Institute for Alternative Journalism, 1992.

Ronald F. Jacobs, *Race, Media, and the Crisis of Civil Society: From the Watts Riots to Rodney King*. Cambridge, UK: Cambridge University Press, 2000.

Norman M. Klein and Martin J. Schiesl, eds., *20th Century Los Angeles: Power, Promotion, and Social Conflict.* Claremont, CA: Regina Books, 1990.

James Kotkin and David Friedman, *The Los Angeles Riots: Causes, Myths and Solutions.* Washington, DC: Progressive Policy Institute, 1993.

Los Angeles Times, Understanding the Riots: Los Angeles Before and After the Rodney King Case. Los Angeles: *Los Angeles Times,* 1992.

Haki R. Madhubuti, ed., *Why L.A. Happened: Implications of the '92 Los Angeles Rebellion.* Chicago: Third World Press, 1993.

Sam March, *A Marxist Defense of the L.A. Rebellion.* New York: World View Forum, 1992.

Tom Owens and Rod Browning, *The Truth Behind the Corruption and Brutality of the L.A.P.D. and the Beating of Rodney King.* New York: Thunder's Mouth Press, 1994.

Manuel Pastor, *Latinos and the Los Angeles Uprising: The Economic Context.* Claremont, CA: The Tomas Rivera Center, 1993.

David Rieff, *Los Angeles, Capital of the Third World.* New York: Simon and Schuster, 1992.

Allen J. Scott and E. Richard Brown, eds., *South Central Los Angeles: Anatomy of an Urban Crisis.* Los Angeles: University of California, Los Angeles, the Lewis Center for Regional Studies, 1993.

Raphael Sonenshein, *Politics in Black and White: Race and Power in Los Angeles.* Princeton, NJ: Princeton University Press, 1993.

Min Hyoung Song, *Strange Future: Pessimism and the 1992 Los Angeles Riots.* Durham, NC: Duke University Press, 2005.

James B. Steinberg, David W. Lyon, and Mary E. Vainana, eds., *Urban America: Policy Choices for Los Angeles and the Nation.* Santa Monica, CA; Rand, 1992.

Bob Vernon, *L.A. Justice.* Colorado Springs, CO: Focus on the Family, 1994.

Michael Wynn, *Enough Is Enough: The Explosion in Los Angeles: America Receives a Wake-Up Call.* Marietta, GA: Rising Sun Publishing, 1993.

Periodicals

Maria Bustillos, "Los Angeles, April 29–May 4, 1992," *The Awl,* August 10, 2011.

Rory Cordell, "Rodney King: 'I Had to Learn to Forgive,'" *Guardian* (UK), May 1, 2012.

Mike Davis, "In L.A., Burning All Illusions: Urban America Sees Its Future," *The Nation,* June 1, 1992.

Mark Fitzgerald, "Coverage Complaints: L.A. Riot Coverage Assignments Frustrated Black Reporters," *Editor & Publisher,* September 19, 1992.

Michael Fumento, "Is the Great Society to Blame? If Not, Why Have Problems Worsened Since '60s," *Investor's Business Daily,* June 19, 1992.

Courtney Garcia, "Ice Cube Reflects on How the LA Riots Changed Rap," thegrio.com, April 29, 2012.

Lewis Gordon, "Of Illicit Appearance: The L.A. Riots/Rebellion as a Portent of Things to Come," truth-out.org, May 12, 2012.

Wendy Greuel, "Wendy Greuel on L.A. Riots: 'We Still Have a Long Way to Go,'" *Daily Beast,* April 26, 2012.

Arsenio Hall, "Arsenio Hall on Filming from L.A. Riots' Ground Zero," *Daily Beast,* April 26, 2012.

Peter Hong, "20 Years After the Riots: A More Worldly Los Angeles, a More Insular *Los Angeles Times,*" *Huffington Post,* May 1, 2012.

Arthur Hu, "Us and Them: An Asian Take on L.A.," *New Republic,* June 1, 1992.

June Jordan, "The Truth of Rodney King," *Progressive,* June 1993.

John Lee, "A Time to Riot: L.A. Uprising 1992," *ColorLines,* Summer 2002.

David A. Love, "LA Riots 20 Years Later: How They Changed the Way We Talk About Race," thegrio.com, April 27, 2012.

Bruce K. MacLaury, "Rediscovering the Common Good," *Brookings Review,* Summer 1992.

Eric Mann, "The Poverty of Corporatism; Los Angeles—A Year After," *The Nation,* March 29, 1993.

Patrick Range McDonald, "Then and Now: Images from the Same Spot as the L.A. Riots, 20 Years Later," *LA Weekly* (microsite), 2012. www.laweekly.com/microsites/la-riots.

The Nation, "City of Ashes," May 25, 1992.

National Review, "Justice Unseen," May 10, 1993.

New Republic, "In Jeopardy," November 15, 1993.

Stephanie O'Neill, "'Get the Hell Out of Here!' (Journalists Attacked During the Los Angeles Riots)," *Columbia Journalism Review,* July–August 1992.

John O'Sullivan, "Riots, Lies, and Videotape," *National Review,* May 25, 1992.

Susan Paterno, "Under Fire: At Hearings on L.A. Riots, Critics Blast Media on Coverage, and Lack of Coverage, of Minorities, Cities," *Editor & Publisher,* August 15, 1992.

Roberto Rodriguez, "The Media, on Trial at Rodney King Trial, Also Guilty," *National Catholic Reporter,* April 30, 1993.

John Rogers and Amy Taxin, "Henry Watson, Man Who Beat Reginald Denny During LA Riots, Says South LA Hasn't Changed," *Huffington Post,* April 25, 2012.

Ted Soqui, "1992 Remembered: A Photographer Follows the Smoke," fryingpannews.org, April 17, 2012.

Dean Takahashi, "The L.A. Riots and Media Preparedness," *Editor & Publisher,* May 23, 1992.

William V. Wenger, "The Los Angeles Riots: A Battalion Commander's Perspective," *Infantry,* January–February 1994.

Charles Whitaker, "The Rodney King Wake-Up Call: Which Way America?," *Ebony,* July 1992.

David Whitman, "The Untold Story of the LA Riots," *U.S. News & World Report,* May 31, 1993.

INDEX